WE SALUTE: • The Past
• The Present
• The Future

Public Service Electric & Gas Co. is proud to have a part in preserving the recorded history of Salem County through presentation of this pictorial.

Through these pages, residents can relive some of their past and re-examine their roots.

It is our hope that this pictorial will inspire readers with a new respect for Salem County's rich history and a recommitment to its future.

PSE&G Nuclear Department employees take great pride in being a part of that commitment.

Nuclear Department
Salem/Artificial Island

Mannington Resilient Floors and its corporate parent, Mannington Mills, Inc., commend Charles Harrison for putting forth his talented time and effort to prepare this pictorial—with the superb quality deserved by Salem County and its industrious people.

Mannington, from its inception in Salem County in 1915 and its unbroken continuation under the ownership and operation by four generations of one local family, recognizes the many advantages of conducting an international manufacturing business that is headquartered in the county.

Salem County's sense of history and continuing tradition, sense of important living values, caring for the past, and the desire for steady improvement and stable growth conspire to offer a special place to live and to work and to build to the future.

While institutions may come and go, it is really the special people who make Salem County the exceptional place that it is. Mannington, at both the institutional and personal levels, is fully dedicated to all the proper pursuits of Salem County and its people.

mannington®
RESILIENT FLOORS

One of Salem County's most revered assets is its history. This rich heritage is the social and cultural foundation upon which the community and its people were pioneered.

Therefore, it is with great pride that Security Savings Bank presents this collection of the history of Salem County.

It is our hope that Salem County: A Story of People will serve as an outstanding contribution toward the preservation of the county's past. Each page brings to life poignant reminders of our beginnings which will undoubtedly help shape our future.

Security is proud to be a part of this legacy and believes that this volume will be cherished by those to whom it is entrusted.

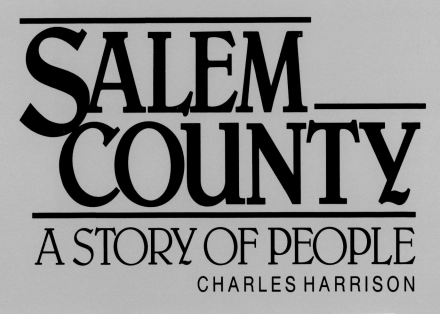

SALEM COUNTY

A STORY OF PEOPLE

CHARLES HARRISON

THE DONNING COMPANY
PUBLISHERS
NORFOLK/VIRGINIA BEACH

The Donning Company/Publishers
Norfolk/Virginia Beach

The Donning Company/Publishers
5659 Virginia Beach Boulevard
Norfolk, Virginia 23502

Edited by Kevin Mitchelle Johnson
Richard A. Horwege, Senior Editor

Library of Congress Cataloging-in-Publication Data

Harrison, Charles Hampton, 1932-
    Salem County: a story of people/by Charles Harrison.
        p.   cm.
    Bibliography: p.
    Includes index.
    ISBN 0-89865-741-5 (lim. ed.)
    1. Salem County (N.J.)—History—Pictorial works. 2. Salem
County (N.J.)—Description and travel—views. I. Title.
F142.S2H37   1988   88-29969
974.9'91—dc 19   CIP

Printed in the United States of America

Contents

Preface

Some counties are known as places where new people have flooded in and covered up most of the roots to the past. Some other counties are places that people move in and out of without leaving much of a trace, and still others are places people cannot wait to leave.

Salem County is not like any of those places. That is because most people who are here have chosen this place, and usually they decide to stay a long while.

Many counties boast that they still have two or three buildings dating back to their and the nation's beginnings. What amazes new Salem County residents and pleases those who have been here a long time is that there are more than one hundred houses in the county that date back two centuries or farther—and they are not museums open to the public one afternoon a week. Families live in them and care for them! And not a few of the owners are descendants of the original owners.

Salem is a county with its roots showing—and proud of it. Yet, the county has been open down through the years to everybody: freed black slaves, Jewish farmers from Russia, Poles and Italians who came in great numbers to work for Du Pont, and migrant workers from Puerto Rico who decided to remain and become part of the permanent population.

This book is about all of these people and more: the Swedish family who suffered the hardships of a cruel Atlantic crossing, only to suffer the hardships of settling a new land; a German button maker who learned glass blowing and started a new industry in America; the man who made Salem County appreciate the tomato and then got the rest of the world to like it; a colonel of American militia who not only defied a British demand for surrender, but called their commander a "barbarous Attila"; and cowboys who ride broncs and wrestle steers every Saturday night in the summer at the only regularly scheduled rodeo east of the Mississippi.

The New Jersey State Museum has a collection of paintings of Lenape Indians by the artists Monte Crews and Kenneth Phillips. In one painting, the Indian hunter has disguised himself to be able to sneak up on his prey. Bows generally were made of hickory or ash, and the arrows were common reeds with a stone point. Construction of a typical Indian house is depicted in the second painting. Green saplings were driven into the ground to give the house support; the tops were then bent and lashed together to form a curved roof. Tree bark was often used for walls and roof.

Photographed by permission from "The Indians of New Jersey: Portfolio of Prints" published in May 1964 by the Archaeological Society of New Jersey

They Who Were Here First

When the streams of Salem County ran swift and pure to the Delaware River and the great ocean beyond, the land belonged to the Lenape Indians. It was theirs for perhaps ten thousand years.

They were a peaceable people, so docile in fact that the warlike Susquehannock tribe to the west, with whom they traded, contemptuously called even their strongest, proudest men women.

The Lenape tribe probably never numbered much more than twelve thousand in all of its territory stretching from southeastern New York State down into northern Delaware. At the turn of the seventeenth century, the Lenape Indians of Salem County were few in number and they lived primarily along those streams that drained the land, and carried fish, clams, and oysters upriver.

Their small villages, smartly built on knolls above the high watermark, contained wood and grass huts. Men, women, and children lived a simple life. They helped themselves to whatever they found in the streams and woods that was tasty and agreeable, and in the seventeenth century they also were growing corn, beans, and squash on small plots.

When a village's residents had depleted the available supply of wood for homes and fires and had farmed the nutrients from the land, a process that might take ten to twenty years, they moved on. They did not have to go far to find another virgin forest or land that had never been turned by an Indian's primitive stone hoe.

Sometimes the Indian families of Salem County and environs followed a trail east to the seashore where they collected shell fish and berries. While they were there, they may have delighted in the fresh sea breezes, and the children may have spent much of their day racing up and down the steep banks of the sand dunes, much as children still do today.

If the Indians drew pictures of each other, they have not survived. White artists and writers who came later painted and described the Lenape man as shaving his head with a sharp flint, except for a strip of hair running back from the forehead. Frank H. Stewart, when he was president of the Gloucester County Historical Society in 1932, wrote that "shocks of hair were left so that there were some half dozen tufts on the head. Each tuft was tied about or braided and was decorated by threading shell wampum at the end of the lock." Feathers of a large bird—perhaps an eagle or osprey—were attached to these clumps of hair. According to Stewart, the shaved portion of the scalp was painted red. Women wore their hair long, sometimes braided and coated with animal fat.

On their bodies, both men and women wore garments made from animal skins. As one would suppose, they wore less in the hot weather. But whatever clothing was worn, it was common to adorn it with wampum—small beads or shells. "The wealth of an Indian was ever apparent in ceremony or the dance by the number of strings of wampum that hung from his neck," wrote Stewart.

Going out for the day's work, the Lenape man carried a bag on his back, according to Stewart, in which he might put food, a clay pipe, tobacco, wampum and trinkets. (Does it sound a little like today's college student going off to classes?) If the day's work included hunting, he also carried bow and arrows in the bag.

Much of what is known today about how the Lenape Indians lived and died in Salem County—before the white man forever changed the old ways—comes from recent archaeological excavations. Because they have never been heavily settled, Salem and neighboring Cumberland County probably have more undisturbed Indian sites than any other county in New Jersey, perhaps more so than any area in all the Lenapes' ancestral territory.

The Lower Delaware Valley Chapter of the Archaeological Society of New Jersey has been excavating Indian sites since 1976. Its members are part-time and self-taught archaeologists—but very dedicated and very hard-working. Some artifacts that have been unearthed have been carbon-dated. A projectile point found several feet down in a farmer's field has been placed in the period 1000 to 2000 B.C.

A recent excavation along Two Penny Run,

The Lenape Indians lived in small villages along the waterways. In other locations, they gathered to process fish that had been caught and nuts that had been gathered. An excavation of just such a "processing" site was begun in 1985 by the Lower Delaware Valley Chapter of the Archaeological Society of New Jersey. In the first picture, William Liebeknecht is measuring the width of an unearthed Indian hearth on which nuts were once boiled in water to extract their oil. The other picture shows Liebeknecht (center) working with his father, Dr. Charles Liebeknecht of Pennsville (right) and Dwayne Bailey, also of Pennsville, screening dirt for artifacts.
Photographs by Stephan Harrison

sandwiched between old U.S. Route 40 and the New Jersey Turnpike, has uncovered the site of a primitive "processing plant."

William Liebeknecht, a former county resident and a professional archaeologist, believes Indians worked at the site to process nuts in the fall and fish in the spring and summer, beginning perhaps four thousand years ago. Pieces of fish and ground nuts were boiled in water over a hearth to get their oil, Liebeknecht believes. Oil was used by the Lenapes to cook their food and soften the animal skins they wore.

George Morris of Penns Grove, owner of a popular take-out restaurant, whose heart is in archaeology, says the diggers of Salem County have found post holes that indicate the location of Indian houses. Extensive house patterns, however, have been obliterated by decades of plowing and by leaching associated with excessive acidity in the soil.

For all the archaeologists of Salem County, amateur and professional alike, their work with shovel, trowel, and hand brush—usually on weekends—eventually causes them to think and feel like those first residents. They begin to ask themselves such questions as, "How far back from the stream would I have built my house?" and "How would I have used this stone implement?"

Said one man as he sat on the edge of a deep hole that uncovered an ancient hearth, "Some Indian sat here several thousand years ago, then got up and never returned." ∎

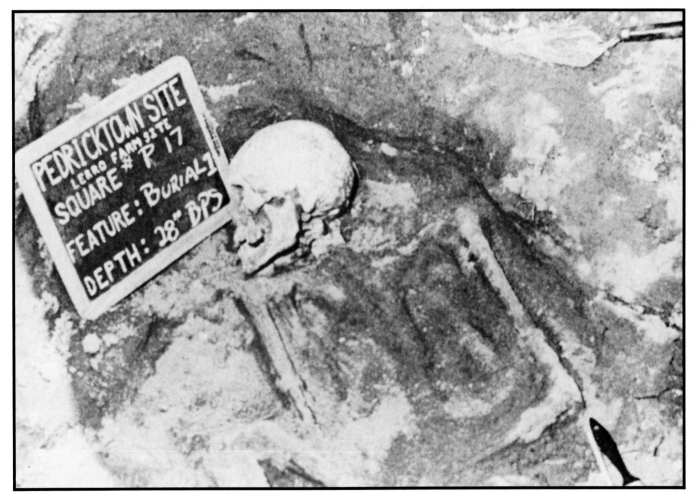

In the early 1970s, the Lower Delaware Valley Chapter of the Archeological Society of New Jersey excavated a Lenape Indian burial site on the Lerro Farm in Pedricktown along the south bank of Oldman's Creek across from Gloucester County. Nine complete and/or partial skeletal remains were unearthed and later reburied. Three were tentatively identified as male and four as female; two could not be determined. Society members noticed that most of the remains were buried in a flexed position, with the knees drawn up. The knee and leg bones can be seen at the bottom of this picture on a direct line below the front of the skull. Photograph used by permission from Bulletin 34 of the Archeological Society of New Jersey published in 1977.

This is one of the agreements signed by settlers and Lenape chiefs whereby the Indians agreed to turn over land in return for small quantities of the white man's guns, clothes, liquor, and trinkets. The date of this agreement is January 4, 1694. The enlargement of the bottom portion of the document shows the marks made by the chiefs. Document from the Salem County Historical Society collection

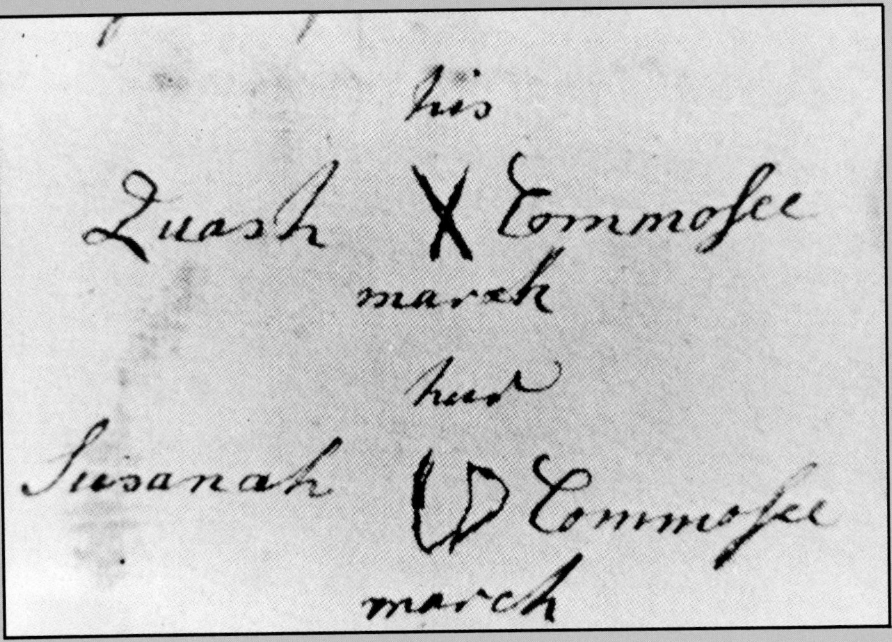

This picture shows the marks made on a document by an Indian husband and wife whose names have been anglicized. Document from the Salem County Historical Society collection

The great Lenape Indian chiefs used marks when signing documents with the white men. This is a later rendition of most of the signs used in the 1600s when the chiefs were selling off land to the early settlers.
Signs from the Salem County Historical Society collection

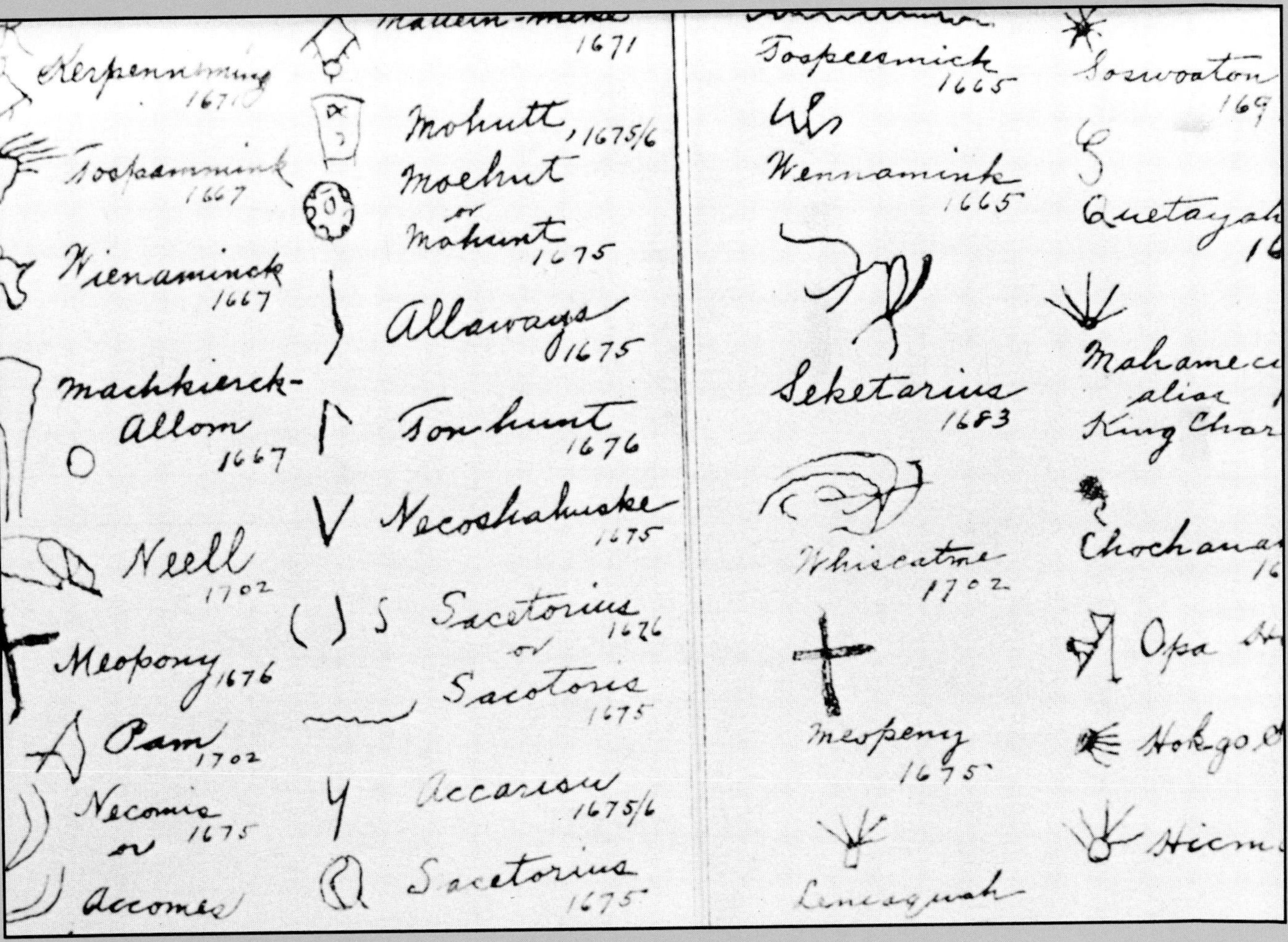

Many houses built two to three hundred years ago still dot the Salem County landscape, and a number of them are noted for the way glazed brick was used in the 1700s for decoration or to inscribe the initials of the original owner(s) and the year when the house was first occupied. William and Mary Oakford built their home south of Alloway in 1736 (W-M-O). In those days, the brick often was made on the home site, and a clay pit existed for many years on the Oakford property. The home has been restored and renovated and is still lived in. Photograph from the Robert P. Dorrell collection

They Who Came By Ship

It was May 20, 1654, when the Swedish ship *Orn* dragged itself, battered and broken, into Fort Christina (near Wilmington, Delaware). It was the last ship to bring emigrants from the fatherland to New Sweden, a small colony of Swedes and Finns that hugged both banks of the Delaware River.

The *Orn* almost did not make it, and nearly a third of its three hundred fifty passengers did not survive the cruel crossing that had begun three and one-half months earlier in Gothenburg, Sweden. Among those who had not died of disease or been swept overboard in one of several violent storms were Nils and Margareta Matson from Torshalla, not far from Stockholm. In the centuries to come, their descendants would bear their children and bury their dead in Salem County.

It is hard for a generation that flies to Europe in a few hours to imagine what it was like for the Swedes, Dutch and English to cross the Atlantic in small wooden sailing ships. Fortunately, Matson left a record of his terrifying voyage, so we have some notion of what he and the early settlers had to endure coming here to start America.

The *Orn* was overcrowded when it left Gothenburg on February 2, 1654, in a "crackling cold" winter storm. The ship was only fifteen days out of port when the captain became lost. When he finally discovered where the ship was, it was off Calais, France.

The captain regained his bearings and set off toward the west, only to run into three British frigates, which proceeded to blow off the *Orn's* bowsprit with their cannon. Their commander also insisted that the *Orn* pull into Dover to get a "passport," presumably to prevent it from being accosted by other ships of the Crown (the crown just then having passed from the executed Charles I and not yet placed upon the head of Charles II). With the passport and additional provisions, the *Orn* pushed off toward the open sea.

The ship ran into another storm, which blew it off course and again confounded the captain. When he recalculated his position this time, he was near the Canary Islands, where he anchored for the night. But no one aboard slept much, because, according to Matson, the natives on shore "shot at us the whole night."

The ship left the islands March 26 and encountered several Turkish ships two weeks later. By this time, disease, some of it caused by eating "rotten victuals" and drinking "putrid water," had ravaged the passengers and crew and thinned their ranks. When the Turkish ships menaced, every man was brought topside and issued a musket.

Those near death were "propped up and supported between two healthy men." The bluff worked, and the Turkish ships sailed away.

The ship bearing those who were dead, dying, or wished they were dead was pounced upon by two more terrible storms that destroyed most of the sails and washed a number of persons overboard. At one point, Matson reported, the wind pushed the ship so far over on its side that the tops of the masts nearly touched the heaving waves.

The *Orn* at last sailed up the Delaware River and past the abandoned Swedish Fort Elfsborg on the shore in Salem County. There was hardly a man aboard who was strong enough to throw the anchor into the river, even among the sailors.

At the time the Matsons disembarked in their new land, the Swedes were only a year away from losing forever their control over the shores of the Delaware. Since the 1630s, when the Swedes first became seriously interested in beaver pelts, tobacco, and empire—perhaps in that order—the Dutch had been either their competitors or partners along the river. When the ships *Kalmar Nyckel* and *Fogel Grip* brought with them in 1638 the Swedes and Finns who would first colonize the Delaware Valley, Dutch investors had nearly a majority interest in the sponsoring agency, the New Sweden Company. The prominent Dutch explorer/trader Peter Minuit was their leader and first governor.

Although its countrymen were prominent in the New Sweden Company, the Dutch government never gave up the dream of firmly planting the Dutch flag all along the shores of the Delaware. (It had established a tenuous foothold in 1630 by building the small Fort Nassau at what is now Gloucester City across from Philadelphia.) In 1644, Johan Printz, the first Swedish governor of New Sweden, reported he was currently on good terms with the Dutch, but noted that Dutch authorities in "Manathans" (New York City) had reminded him of "the pretension of the Dutch West India Company to this entire river."

Peter Stuyvesant, the one-legged governor of New Amsterdam, acted on the pretension in September 1655. His superior force first persuaded the Swedes to surrender Fort Casimir in Delaware (which they had previously taken from the Dutch).

Then he crossed the river to Salem County and landed several hundred soldiers at Fort Elfsborg, which the Swedes had given up several years before when they occupied Fort Casimir (and gladly left, by all accounts, because the mosquitoes were so fierce the soldiers had renamed the place "Mygeenborg," or gnat fort).

Stuyvesant and his men marched around vigorously and thundered their cannon repeatedly, and the tour de force was sufficient to intimidate the Swedes. Thus, New Sweden, but not the Swedish families, disappeared.

The Dutch influence was not destined to last long because the English had pretensions of their own.

Actually, a small band of English puritans had settled along Salem Creek (then known as Varkens Kill) in about 1641. Because they came to Salem County from New Haven, Connecticut, they were known as the New Haven colony. These settlers probably never numbered more than one hundred persons, and when Printz was governor of New Sweden, they swore allegiance to Queen Christina. Mainly as the result of disease, the New Haven Colony was nearly wiped out by the time Stuyvesant

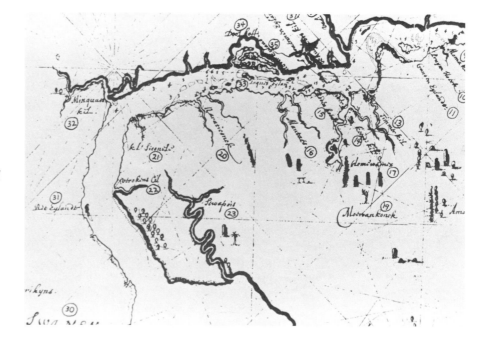

This is a portion of an old Dutch map showing Salem County and environs. The map was drawn in the early seventeenth century. At the lower left can be seen the word Swanen. Swanen Dael *was the Dutch name for the state of Delaware. What appears to be* Varkins Kill, *the Dutch name for the Salem River, is located just above the cluster of trees at left center.*
Map from the Salem County Historical Society collection

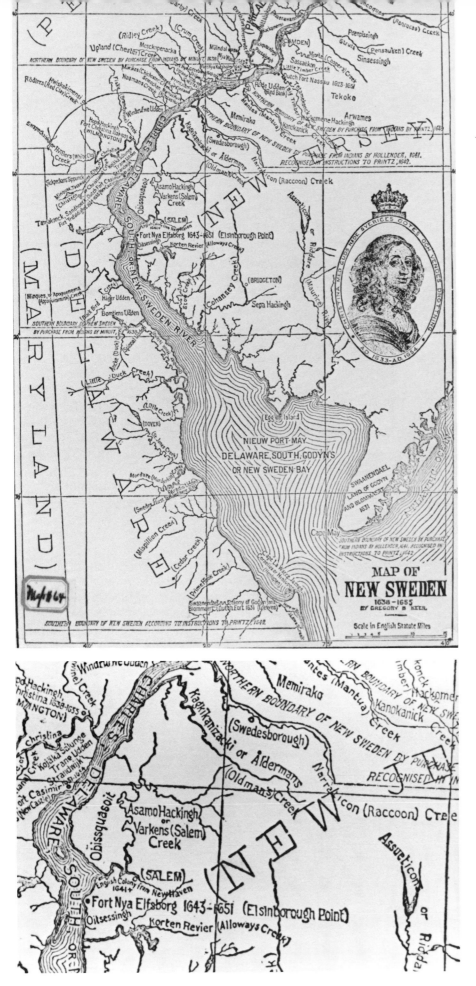

The map shows New Sweden along both banks of the Delaware River in the period 1638 and 1655. The map maker is Gregory B. Keen. Some of the landmarks shown in the enlargement of the Salem County area and their later English names are as follows: Fort Nya Elfsborg (Elsinboro Point), Korten Revier (Alloways Creek), Varkens Revier (Salem Creek), and Obissquasoit (Penns Neck). The latter name, of course, is in the Lenape Indian language, not Swedish.
Map from the Salem County Historical Society collection

came along and made the survivors citizens of the Netherlands.

With Charles II on the throne, the British Empire decided to move in on the Dutch in 1664, and the rest is history—English history that is, up to 1776.

We think of George Washington as the father of our country, and Maj. John Fenwick (an officer in Cromwell's army) must certainly be considered the father of Salem County. Unlike Washington, however, Fenwick's reputation suffered from a good deal more than a chopped-down-cherry-tree incident.

Till his death, Fenwick maintained he was the innocent victim of some sordid wheeling and dealing by fellow Quakers. He may have been right, but today he would be considered to be at the very least a land speculator of the first order.

In 1673, the British colony of New Jersey was divided along a line that roughly ran from above the Delaware Water Gap southeast to a point near Tuckerton on the coast.

West Jersey had been given to John Lord Berkeley by King Charles II, and Lord Berkeley was willing to sell it for one thousand pounds. Fenwick was anxious to buy, but he didn't have the money. Like any good speculator, he borrowed what he needed. The lender was fellow Quaker Edward Byllynge. Unfortunately, Byllynge owed money himself and really could not afford to loan Fenwick one thousand pounds. When Byllynge's creditors found out about the loan to Fenwick, the deal fell through. The matter was put to arbitration before William Penn, who decided that Byllynge was not entitled to loan Fenwick that much money. In the end, Fenwick was able to buy only one-tenth of West Jersey. His purchase consisted of present-day Salem and Cumberland counties. Of course, even then it was not a final sale because Fenwick still had to negotiate with the Lenape Indians who occupied the land and, naturally, had not been consulted, but more about that shortly.

Still in London, Fenwick began buying supplies for his own family and perhaps others who accompanied him to his new land. However, Fenwick still was short of hard cash, so he charged most of what he purchased. The tradesmen, figuring (probably correctly) that they might never get paid if Fenwick remained in New Jersey, threatened to throw him into debtor's prison if he did not pay up before embarkation.

In desperation, Fenwick turned once again to fellow Quakers, John Eldridge and Edmund Warner. They agreed to pay off his debts in exchange for their holding a mortgage on Salem and Cumberland counties.

Again, the Friends turned out not to be very good friends. Fenwick learned after he had arrived in New Jersey that Eldridge and Warner had never paid off his debts and, furthermore, were circulating the story in London that Fenwick did not really own any land because they held the mortgage. The scandal was to hound Fenwick all of his days.

Fenwick and forty-nine other persons, including three daughters and two sons-in-law, arrived in the land he sort of owned aboard the ship *Griffin* on September 23, 1675. He called it New Salem because it seemed a peaceful place.

Thirteen Indian chiefs, some of whom no doubt had previously "sold" the fields and forests to the Dutch and Swedish, now handed over all of Salem and Cumberland counties to Fenwick for four guns (with lead and powder), ten and one-half ankers of rum (approximately 336 gallons), four blankets, sixteen match coats, and assorted other clothing and goods.

Perhaps to raise much-needed capital, Fenwick had, while still in England, sold some parcels of land in his colony to persons who sailed with him aboard the *Griffin*. Now, he sold more acreage and also gave away land to family members, including his daughter Priscilla, who married one of the ship's passengers, James Champneys.

Fenwick reserved six thousand acres for himself, and the property became known as Fenwick's Grove.

The *Griffin* returned in 1676 with more emigrants, and the ships continued to arrive regularly thereafter for many years.

It is estimated by the Salem County Historical Society that descendants of more than half of those English settlers of the late 1600s and early 1700s still reside in Salem County.

Fenwick would be pleased. ∎

In 1988, New Jersey and Pennsylvania celebrated the three hundred fiftieth anniversary of the establishment of a Swedish colony along both shores of the Delaware River. In commemoration of the event, the New Sweden Company, a modern successor to Peter Minuit's New Sweden Company of 1637, built a model seventeenth-century Swedish village in the city park of Bridgeton (Cumberland County). By using skilled craftsmen from Sweden and importing many household and farm implements from Sweden, the company was able to maintain authenticity. Visitors to the village were able to learn what life was like in the colony as it existed in Salem, Cumberland, and Gloucester counties. The first picture shows the village well. The bucket was easily lowered and raised by using the handle partially seen at the right of the picture. More than eight hundred trees were felled to supply logs for seven buildings in the village, including the enkelstuga (residence) shown in the second picture.

The log cabin typically had two rooms and a fireplace; very often there was a sod roof, such as the one shown here. The typical Swedish house of the time had the fireplace in the corner of the room, and it was elevated two or three feet off the floor. One advantage of such a fireplace over the later English colonial fireplace, which was at floor level, was that Swedish women's skirts were less likely to catch on fire. Photographs by Stephan Harrison

21

Ragnhild Holm, who emigrated from Sweden in the 1950s, was one of the guides at the New Sweden exhibit. In the first picture, she describes one building that served two purposes: rokhus *(smokehouse) and* badstuga *(bathhouse). It was when people took their sauna, of course, that the building became a bathhouse. The Swedish family used the sauna at least once a week until the English took control of New Jersey in 1664. "We were a clean people until the English convinced us not to bathe so often," said Mrs. Holm. In the second picture, Mrs. Holm sharpens an axe blade, and in the third picture she shows early farm implements that were made from tree saplings and branches. The final picture is a one-room, rough-hewn cabin that a family might live in while building something better.*
Photographs by Stephan Harrison

This is an old Swedish house built in the 1600s and still standing on the grounds of the Hancock house in Lower Alloways Creek. The second picture shows how the Swedes cut their logs in such a way as to allow them to interlock snugly and permanently at the corners of the house.
Photographs from the Salem County Historical Society collection

The Swedish engineer Peter Martensson Lindstrom visited New Sweden in 1633 and drew this map of the colony and this version of the Lenape Indians he saw. Some of the Swedish families he might have encountered are Bengtssen, Garretson, Jonasson, Mollicka, Pehrssen and Van Jumme. Lindstrom reported that the Salem County marshes were "stinking and unhealthy." He no doubt had heard all the complaints about the mosquitoes.

Photographs reprinted from the Summer 1987 issue of South Jersey Magazine

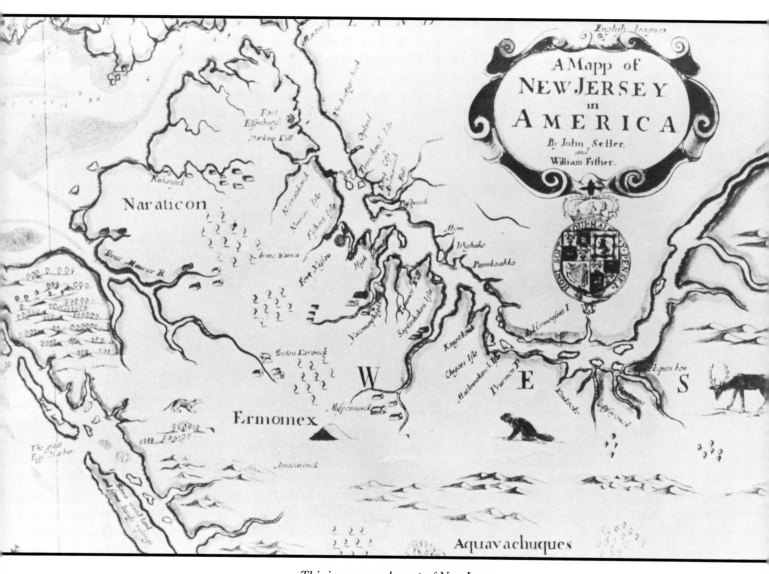

This is a very early map of New Jersey by John Seller and William Fisher. In the way it has been drawn, the state has been laid on its side so that you are reading the map from east to west rather than south to north. To get a more familiar view of New Jersey, turn the page so that the left side of the picture is at the bottom. The only Salem County landmarks shown are Varkins Kill, the Dutch name for the Salem River, and the Swedish Fort Elfsborg.

Map from the Salem County Historical Society collection

No one is exactly sure what the Swedish Fort Elfsborg looked like, but William Nelson Brown of Salem probably knows as much about the fort as anyone. Brown is a descendant of the Matson family, which arrived on the last ship to New Sweden in 1654. He painstakingly researched seventeenth-century forts in preparation for building a scale model of the fort to honor the 350th anniversary of the first settlement of Swedes and Finns along the Delaware River in 1638. It took Brown three months of mostly twelve-hour days to build the model of the fort, which was displayed in the spring of 1988. In one picture, Brown, who went to all the trouble for the express purpose of instructing young people, describes his work to Scott Tupper, fourteen, who came with his art teacher to view the exhibit. The other pictures show the fort from different angles. The gun mounts are made of mahogany. Sculptor Molly Carpenter of Salem made the clay figures. Brown said the materials cost him eight hundred dollars.
Photographs by Stephan Harrison

John Pledger may have arrived in
Salem County ahead of John Fenwick.
At least he was not listed as a passenger
aboard the ship, Griffin, that brought
Fenwick and his first settlers in 1675.
However, Pledger's wife, Elizabeth,
and his son, Joseph, who was almost
four years old, are listed. In any event,
one of Fenwick's early land grants as
Lord Proprietor of the colony was to
John and Elizabeth Pledger. This deed
is for three thousand acres.
Deed from the Salem County Historical
Society collection.

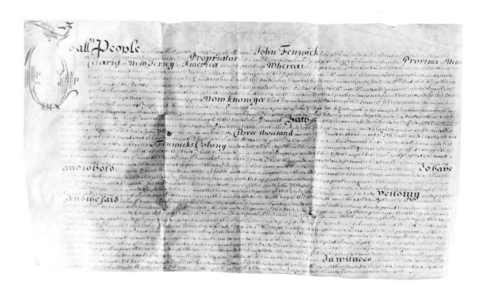

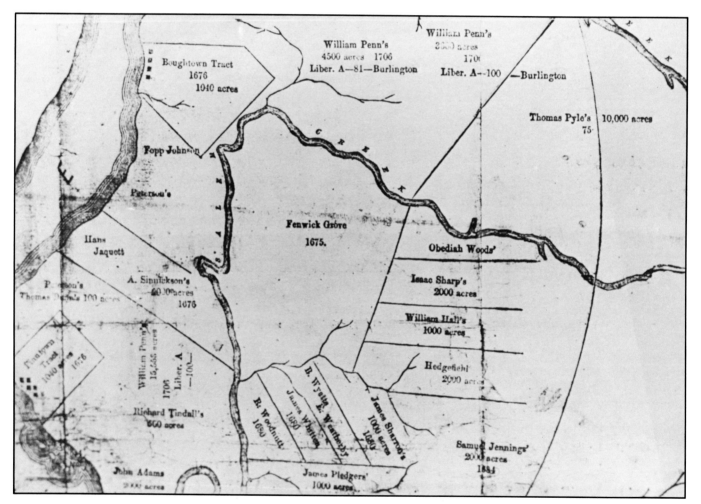

The nineteenth century historian
Thomas Shourds of Salem County
drew a map of the county showing the
acreage given to early settlers in John
Fenwick's colony. Shourds's map was
based on his study of seventeenth-
century land surveys. This portion of
his map shows, for example, Fenwick's
Grove (center) along Salem Creek,
and land that passed into the hands of
William Penn (top border in what is
now Gloucester County). The ten thousand acres deeded to Thomas Pyle
(upper righthand corner) became Pilesgrove Township.
Map from the Salem County
Historical Society collection

I *Preston Carpenter* of the *township of Mannington in the County of Salem*
do hereby set free from bondage, my *Negro boy Wiltshire*
when *he* shall arrive at the age of *twenty one* years which will be on the
twentyeth day of the *third* month, anno Domini, one thousand
seven hundred *and Eighty five* and do, for myself, my executors and
administrators, release unto the said *Wiltshire ᴀ ᴀ ᴀ* all my right,
and all claim whatsoever as to *his* person, or to any estate *he* may ac-
quire, hereby declaring the said *Negro Wiltshire ᴀ ᴀ ᴀ ᴀ* absolutely
free, without any interruption from me, or any person claiming under
me. In witness whereof I have hereunto set my hand and seal this *forth*
ᴀ ᴀ day of the *first* month, in the year of our Lord, one thousand
seven hundred and *Eighty Seventy Eight*

Sealed and delivered }
in the Presence of }
William Goodwin
Jn.º Goodwin

Preston Carpenter

.11

William Patterson, first president of the
Salem County Historical Society,
painted John Fenwick's original home
at Ivey Point based on his father's
memory of the house and grounds. The
house was torn down in 1831. Ivey
Point was located on Fenwick's Creek
west of the present-day Market Street
bridge in Salem. The painting hangs in
a second floor room at the Society's
museum on Market Street.
Painting from the Salem County
Historical Society collection

In the year 1778, settler Preston
Carpenter signed an official document
in which he pledged to set free his Negro
slave, Wiltshire, when the boy reached
the age of twenty-one in the year 1785.
Document from the Salem County
Historical Society collection

Two major incidents occurred in Salem County during the Revolutionary War, both taking place in March 1778. On the eleventh of that month, approximately one thousand British soldiers under the command of Col. Charles Mawhood left Philadelphia for Salem County to forage for cattle, horses, and foodstuff. Mawhood made his headquarters in the city of Salem, and the foraging began on the seventeenth at the farms north of Alloways Creek in Elsinboro and Mannington. The local militia were determined to prevent the British from foraging south of Alloways Creek—so they guarded Quinton, Thompson's, and Hancock's bridges. On the eighteenth, an advance party of the British Seventeenth Infantry Regiment reported the militia's defense line on the south side of Quinton's bridge and expressed fear the Americans, whom they thought to have superior manpower, might cross the bridge and attack them. This rendering of the old wooden drawbridge at Quinton, which separated the two forces on March 18, 1778, was made in 1971 by a local student, Wesley Saunderline.

Drawing reprinted from the Quinton Township centennial booklet published in 1973

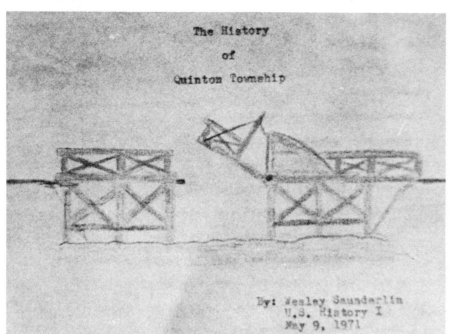

3

They Who First Called Themselves Americans

In 1708, British subject John Hancock—descendant of Englishman William Hancock, Sr.—who had come to Fenwick's Colony with his wife in 1677, built a bridge across Alloways Creek, a stream named for one of the great Lenape chiefs. Seventy years later, British and tory soldiers came across that bridge and killed John's son, William, an American.

The eighteenth century in Salem County was marked by the birth of a prosperous glassblowing industry. Many residents were increasingly aware that they were estranged from a distant king and parliament, and were concerned about the death of patriots killed close to home, sometimes by their neighbors.

This part of South Jersey contains two natural ingredients that early farmers and industrialists considered valuable: marl to neutralize the acid in the soil and sand for making glass. Marl, sometimes referred to as green goo, now mostly impedes the drilling of modern wells, but farmers once put it on their fields for the same reason their twentieth century descendants spread lime.

Caspar Wistar, who emigrated to this country from Germany in 1717, was among the first entrepreneurs to appreciate the quality of our fine, white sand. On a cold January day in 1783, Wistar, who had been making brass buttons in Philadelphia, purchased one hundred plus acres of woodland a few miles northeast of Alloway for a glassmaking plant. Unfortunately, he did not know much about making glass, so, while he was clearing his land and laying out buildings, he hired four experienced glass blowers from Holland to come over and give him lessons and to get the new business underway.

Wistar was a fast learner, and so was his son, Richard, who took over the business from his father in 1752. By the year 1760, the Wistar Glass Manufactory employed fifty or sixty men, a very large number for an industry of that day, and had expanded its facilities to cover more than one thousand acres. Indeed, the company was such a thriving business that the Wistars created the company town of—what else—Wistarburgh, which had its company store and company housing. Community gatherings, including parties and dances, took place in the company's warehouse.

The company was known far and wide for its expertly blown glassware in such colors as sea green, golden amber, and smoky brown. But its big business was supplying window glass for the many new homes of clapboard, brick, and sandstone that were built primarily along the same waterways where the Lenape Indians once lived in their small villages.

An ad for the company in a 1769 issue of the *Pennsylvania Gazette* referred to "between 300 and 400 boxes of window glass consisting of common sizes...or any uncommon sizes under 16 x 18...."

Richard Wistar also bragged in the ad that all glass was of "American manufacture." He went on to say that "America ought also encourage her own manufacture." The latter statement probably was in response to Parliament's imposition of a duty on glass exported to the colonies.

The Wistar Glass Manufactory flourished until the early 1780s when the worsening economic condition caused by the Revolutionary War forced the company to close down.

The Salem County residents who, before the war, bought Wistar window glass and Wistar jars and bottles included, of course, descendants of the early Swedish and English Quaker settlers. But now there also were Germans, French Huguenots, black slaves, Belgians, Scots, and English who were not Quakers. Down the road from a Friends meeting house or a Swedish Lutheran church might be a congregation of Baptists, Methodists, Presbyterians, or Episcopalians (Church of England). Roman Catholics, many of whom worked for Wistar, met secretly in homes because English law forbade them to worship in public.

The first meeting house of the Society of Friends was a log cabin built close by an oak tree that stood singularly tall and many-boughed along Wharf Street (now Broadway) in Salem.

The initial meeting was held on the last day of May in 1676. Those present, who included John Fenwick, decided to meet monthly thereafter "to consider. . .outward circumstances and business." Furthermore, any of their number who had "walked disorderly" would be "admonished, exhorted, and also reproved, and their evil deeds and practices testified against in the wisdom of God and in the authority of truth."

By 1765, the Society of Friends had established three other meetings, at Alloway, Hancock's Bridge, and Pilesgrove-Woodstown.

The Swedish Lutherans had, up until the early 1700s, generally worshipped across the river in Delaware. But it was a hazardous crossing three hundred years ago. As a result, two congregations were formed on this side of the river, one in Gloucester County and the other at Penns Neck (now Pennsville).

In 1715, the Penns Neck congregation engaged a German by the name of Regner von Aist to help them build a church measuring twenty-four feet square, for which he was paid twenty-four pounds (apparently one pound per foot). He was assisted in the work by

Colonel Mawhood and Maj. John G. Simcoe arrived on the scene with reinforcements and then devised a plan to lure the American militia over the bridge and into an ambush. A company of British soldiers formed on the road leading back to Salem and, in full view of the militia, began what appeared to be a retreat. But the main body of redcoats were hidden in the nearby Weatherby house and on its grounds. The militia, under the command of Capt. William Smith, took the bait. The British plan worked, and the militia were surprised and driven back across the bridge with a loss of six men (one drowned in the creek). The British were prevented from crossing the bridge and inflicting more casualties by the arrival of militiamen from Cumberland County. Captain Smith, who was wounded in the engagement, lived a long life, dying in 1820 at the age of seventy-eight. He lies buried in what is now a small national cemetery in Quinton just north on the Jericho Road from the house where he lived. Also buried there are militiamen killed at Quinton's Bridge and other Revolutionary War veterans.
Photographs by Stephan Harrison

members of the congregation, including Jean Jaquet, Jacob von Devair, Jan Minck, Lucas Peterson, John von Neeman, and Jacob Hindersson.

God may have filled their heart, but their mind sometimes was on other things, like who was supposed to sit in which pew.

At a parish meeting on the sixth day of January in 1729, it was discovered that some members had been sitting in the wrong pew for a very long time. A few persons were so upset by this disclosure that they boycotted church services for more than a year and refused to help pay the rector's salary, which amounted to a mere pittance anyway.

Thirteen years later, the congregation adopted the rites of the Church of England, which, before the end of the century, became the Protestant Church (now St. George's Episcopal Church on North Broadway in the long shadow of the Delaware Memorial Bridge).

The Reverend Samuel Eakin, who became pastor of the Penn's Neck Presbyterian Church in 1773, was passionate for God and America. He was described as a great preacher and patriot, who wielded considerable influence over his flock and the community at large. Whenever the militia trained, Mr. Eakin was on hand to exhort and encourage the men. It was said they idolized him, were roused by his patriotic zeal, and were ready to lay down their lives for him.

According to the 1920 Almanac published by the First National Bank of Woodstown, Mr. Eakin remained until shortly after the signing of the Declaration of Independence, at which time, "having rendered himself obnoxious to the tories by his zeal in the cause of American liberty, he was compelled to withdraw and return to a church in the New Castle [Delaware] Presbytery."

The tension in the Penn's Neck Presbyterian Church was typical of what prevailed throughout the county in the decade or so preceding the Revolutionary War, during it, and for as long after as it took to heal the terrible hurts inflicted by one resident upon another.

An early lightning rod who deservedly absorbed many of the charges levelled against Mother England by the people who first called themselves Americans was John Hatton, collector of customs for the port of Salem. Ironically, Hatton replaced Samuel Hopkinson, who later was a signer of the Declaration of Independence and a member of the Constitutional Convention.

Historian Joseph S. Sickler calls Hatton "one of the most unpopular men of this period. He seems to have made everybody angry and, as far as Salem County was concerned, became a contributing source

to the Revolution." People found him to be overbearing, insolent, and unscrupulous—for starters.

Hatton brought legal action against several prominent Salem County residents, claiming they had abused him and his office. Even the loyalist government threw out the charges and instead warned Hatton to improve his own disposition and manner. The record would indicate that he never did become anything more than a thoroughly despised representative of King George.

As war with England threatened, Hatton got out of Salem (or maybe he was forced out), and he lived briefly in Swedesboro. But he was no more popular there than he was here. Perhaps sensing that his time was running out among the patriots, Hatton at last joined the British army.

It was easy for Salem County patriots to say good riddance to Hatton, because he never was truly a neighbor. But it must have been very difficult to learn that friends, perhaps relatives, had joined either the British regulars or, what was more likely, one of the tory regiments formed in the state. The very worst blow of all, one supposes, would be to discover that someone you knew or knew about had become a spy for British raiding parties—parties that sometimes killed and maimed innocents.

At least four tory men were convicted of high treason and sentenced to hang. They later were pardoned on condition that they leave the state within two months and the country within six months. Perhaps the most notorious local tory of all was Hugh Cowperthwaite of Pittsgrove, who guided marauding British troops under Col. Charles Mawhood and Maj. John Graves Simcoe. He left the county before he could be apprehended. However, his property was later confiscated, along with that of other convicted tories.

Salem County's Quaker men were caught between the proverbial rock and hard place. If they agreed to join the militia and take up arms against the British, and some did, they often were disowned by their pacifist brethren in the Society of Friends. On the other hand, if they refused to join the militia, and many did out of religious conviction, they often were fined for violating state law that required all able-bodied men to serve in one of the four New Jersey regiments.

Throughout the Revolution, Salem County served as a larder for both armies. The local farmers had done their work well; the fields produced bountiful crops, the cows produced sweet milk, and the livestock grew choice and plump.

During the terrible winter at Valley Forge, Gen. Anthony Wayne and a detachment of American troops crossed the Delaware River into Salem County to round up whatever livestock they could find, drive them north, and ferry them across the river to feed Washington's starving soldiers. They collected about 150 head, and some historians credit the Salem County cattle with saving the army at Valley Forge—and perhaps much more.

Most of the patriot blood shed in Salem County during the war was that of American soldiers and local militia men. They were trying to prevent the British from taking away everything they could lay their hands on.

Alloways Creek was, and still is, a natural boundary separating the southern quarter of the county from the remainder. The Americans thought they could defend the farms and people of that portion of the county by making a stand at the creek. The battles at Quinton's Bridge and Hancock's Bridge were the consequence.

It was because of the men who took up their muskets and laid down their life along Alloways Creek, and patriots like them, that Salem entered the nineteenth century secure as a county of the state of New Jersey in the United States of America.

The British foraging parties continued their plunder north of Alloways Creek on March nineteenth and twentieth, but Colonel Mawhood was incensed that his forces had not been able to cross the creek and raid the prosperous farms in the southern part of the county. Therefore, he planned a surprise attack on the militiamen guarding Hancock's Bridge before dawn on the twenty-first. During the day on the twentieth, the redcoats marched back and forth on the north side of the creek as if to taunt and intimidate the Americans, who could see them plainly from the opposite bank. That night, soldiers from the British Twenty-seventh Regiment took over the Abbott house (picture one), which is across Alloways Creek from the William Hancock house. They imprisoned the William Abbott family in their attic. Also during the night, Major Simcoe and his rangers landed in the marshes two miles below the Hancock house, where the Americans were quartered for the night, and marched through mud and water up to their knees. Before dawn, the rangers approached the Hancock house (picture two) and killed the American sentries before they could sound an alarm. Then they divided their force, with half going to the rear of the house and half to the front and back doors (picture three) and entered the main room of the house (picture four).
Photographs by Stephan Harrison, except picture four, which is reproduced from a postcard.

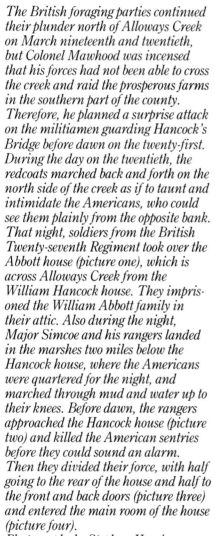

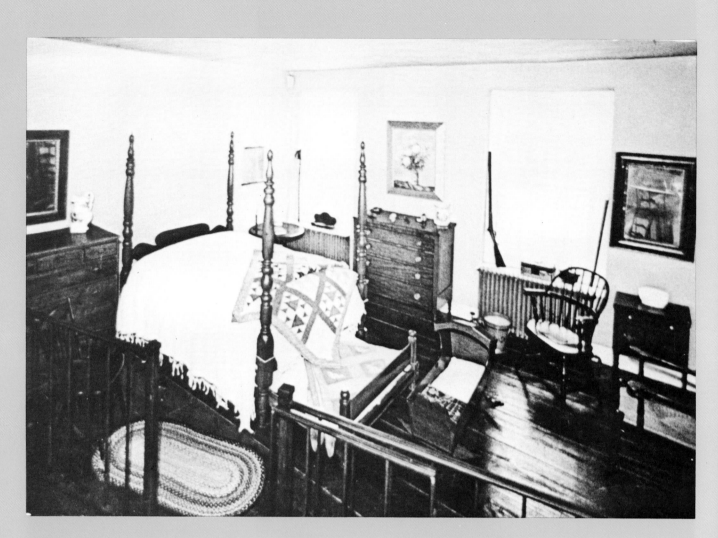

Roused from sleep, the Americans, who numbered about twenty, were defenseless. All but one were bayoneted and killed or mortally wounded. One man is said to have escaped. Also killed was the elderly William Hancock, who was asleep in his bed (picture five). As dawn was beginning to break, the Abbott family in their home across the creek (picture six) looked out the window at the east end of the attic, where the British soldiers continued to hold them (picture seven), and saw the aftermath of the bloody attack. A marker in the Canton Baptist Church cemetery honors the burial place of some of the men killed in the Hancock house (picture eight).
Photographs by Stephan Harrison, except picture five, which is reproduced from a postcard

HONOR TO THE BRAVE AMERICAN
PATRIOTS KILLED IN THE
MASSACRE AT HANCOCK'S BRIDGE
MARCH 21, 1778.
ERECTED MAY 19, 1928.

Later in the day of the twenty-first, Colonel Mawhood, perhaps believing the massacre of the sleeping Americans could lead to the end of resistance in Salem County, wrote this ultimatum intended for Elijah Hand and Benjamin Holme, commanders of the Cumberland and Salem County militias, and about sixteen other prominent patriots. Claiming he was "induced by motives of humanity," Mawhood offered to withdraw his troops from the area if the militiamen would surrender their arms and stay at home. If the militiamen did not accept his offer, Mawhood threatened, he would organize local tories into marauding bands that would destroy the homes and property of militiamen and other patriots "and reduce them, their unfortunate wives and children to beggary and distress. . . ." Colonels Hand and Holme and the other patriots named would be "the first objects to feel the vengeance of the British nation," Mawhood warned. Actually, British soldiers already had partially burned the house of Colonel Holme and destroyed or carried off most of the household possessions and farm animals. In his response to Mawhood, Colonel Hand first referred to the "butchering" of Americans who had surrendered to the British at Quinton's Bridge and to the massacre "in cold blood" of defenseless men in the Hancock house. He concluded: "Your proposal, that we should lay down our arms, we absolutely reject. We have taken them up to maintain rights which are dearer to us than our lives." Document from the Salem County Historical Society collection

38

It is said that some of the last remaining Lenape Indians in Salem County worshipped here in the Old Pittsgrove Presbyterian Church in Daretown, which was built in 1767. The congregation had been meeting in a log church since 1741, but they felt they had outgrown that building. At a congregational meeting on November 14, 1765, the families assembled stated they were "convinced that God in his providence is now inviting us to build for Him a New House and decent house for public worship." On the same property as the church stands today a replica of a log school (second and third pictures), which became known as the Pittsgrove Log College, although it offered only elementary level instruction. The school was built shortly after the log church, and its first teachers were the church's pastors. One of the school's prize pupils was Robert G. Johnson, the man who later introduced Salem County to the tomato.
Photographs by Stephan Harrison

The Nieukirk family were early settlers in the eastern part of Salem County and pillars of the Old Pittsgrove Presbyterian Church. The emigrants and most of their descendants are buried in the church's cemetery. Col. Cornelius Nieukirk commanded one of two companies of militia formed from among members of the church. His men helped Gen. Anthony Wayne drive Salem County cattle north in 1778 to feed Washington's starving men at Valley Forge. The framed picture is of the Reverend George W. Janvier, who served as church pastor from 1812 to 1857. He may hold the record for longest tenure of any pastor in any church at any time in the county. He died June 9, 1865, at the age of eighty-two and is buried in the church cemetery. A resolution passed by the church's session at the time of his death declared the congregation would "always cherish his memory in our hearts as having been a faithful servant, devoted expounder of the lively oracles of God, [and] as having...led us into green pastures and beside the still waters...."

Photographs by Stephan Harrison

Since 1933, an annual memorial service has been held in the Old Pittsgrove Presbyterian Church. Regular weekly worship services and other church activities have been conducted in the nearby Pittsgrove Presbyterian Church since it was built to replace the old edifice toward the end of the Civil War. The fifty-fifth service was conducted in the old restored church on June 5, 1988. Following tradition, the congregation was called to worship by the sounding of a conch shell. Madelynne Ware, shown in the first picture, has been sounding the shell for the last four years. She is a direct descendant of Louis Du Bois, a charter member of the old church and an American officer during the Revolutionary War. The next three pictures are of the worship service. Photographs by Stephan Harrison

In colonial times, mile markers were placed along old King's Highway between Salem and Camden. Each marker told the number of miles from (or to) each city. Most of the markers north of the Salem County line are long gone, but some of the original stones can be seen on the stretch of road from Route 40 south to the Woodstown-Salem Road.
Photographs by Stephan Harrison

Pole Tavern was a licensed tavern thirty-six years before the Declaration of Independence was signed, but it got its name from the liberty pole that was erected outside at the outbreak of the War of 1812. The tavern stood approximately where Routes 40 and 77 intersect in Upper Pittsgrove Township. It was destroyed by fire in April 1918.
Photograph from the Jay Williams collection

43

Farming in Salem County usually has involved the whole family. Charles Holladay and his family in Lower Alloways Creek are shown here in the *early 1900s gathering in the hay, although one wonders whether the children sitting on the ground are primarily engaged in woolgathering.* *Photograph by William J. S. Bradway from the Lower Alloways Creek collection*

They Who Made The Land Prosper

When, in 1820, Col. Robert G. Johnson lauded the benefits of eating the tomato, the people of Salem County thought he was crazy. Everybody knew that lycopersicon esculentum was a poisonous fruit.

So much for folk wisdom.

Not only did the tomato turn out to be nonfatal and good-tasting, it also was destined to be very good for the economy of the county. Perhaps only DuPont has had greater impact.

But before Colonel Johnson and the tomato, there was trouble in the land. Part of the problem was in the soil itself. It was worn out. Crop rotation was still unknown, and marl, which contained lime and potash, while plentiful in underground deposits was still not fully appreciated for its ability to enrich the soil when spread as fertilizer.

The other part of the problem was in the new nation. At the end of the Revolutionary War, the United States owed foreign governments, particularly France, $12 million. The domestic debt was in the amount of $42 million, one-third of it being accrued interest. Whatever the economists of that day called their times, today's experts and pundits would say the country was in the throes of a depression.

When the Lenape Indians had exhausted their small plots of ground, they had simply packed up and moved on to fresh soil. In the early years of the nineteenth century, a number of Salem County residents followed the Indians' example. They abandoned their failing farms and headed west—to the frontier won in war or purchased by treaty. Great grandchildren of the county's early settlers now became the settlers of America beyond the Appalachians.

In 1803, Zadock Street of Salem, New Jersey, founded a new town in Ohio and named it—what else—Salem. Susan Yorke and her family made their way to the Tennessee Valley, where she later married Andrew Donaldson Jackson, adopted son of President Jackson. A descendant of Christopher White, who had come here soon after Fenwick, navigated the Ohio River in a flatboat and lived to write about it.

Those farming families who remained behind and stuck it out through the mean, lean years of the late 1700s and early 1800s eventually were rewarded. For starters, Judge William Hancock, a descendant of the William Hancock who was mortally wounded in his home by the British in 1778, and others finally perceived the qualities of the marl that had been underfoot but underused for so long. Also, farmers had attained greater knowledge about getting the most from the land without depleting its nutrients.

Then there was the steamboat. By the 1830s, steamboats were running regularly between the port of Salem and Philadelphia. The ships brought in goods and new residents, but, more importantly, they took to market the fruits of those who labored in

Salem County's fields and small industries.

All of these developments were abetted by the Salem County Agricultural Association, which was established in 1826 by none other than the same Colonel Johnson who saved the reputation of the tomato, about which more will be said later.

One day in 1840, while things were looking up for the residents of Fenwick's former colony, a group of strange men on horseback rode through Salem and crossed the line into Cumberland County. When they returned, they had with them eleven black men, women, and children—all of them in chains. The strange men were Maryland slaveholders, and they had found and captured their runaway slaves.

However, more often than not in those decades just before the Civil War, slaveholders who crossed the Delaware River in search of their "property" came up empty. The reason was the homes of a number of county residents, most of them Quakers who had long opposed slavery, were stations on the underground railroad helping black slaves escape to freedom.

One stop was the Quaker George Abbott's Tide Mill Farm on the south shore of Salem River in Mannington. In a history of the Abbott family, George's granddaughter, Ruth, wrote that her father (also named George) was a boy "playing in the barnyard when he happened upon a Negro slave. He was hiding in the haymow with just his head protruding. Young George became very excited and ran to his father exclaiming, 'Daddy, Daddy, I just saw a black man out in the haymow!' His father calmly answered, 'Son, just forget thee saw anything.'"

Slavery was supposedly ended in New Jersey by the Constitution of 1844 (in a later decision, the state's supreme court found the Constitution somewhat vague on the status of slavery). However, black men—and women—had been voting for years because of the fuzzy language in the Constitution of 1776.

In 1849, free blacks in Salem and Gloucester counties, led by John S. Rock of Salem, petitioned the state legislature to give them the right to vote. The petitioners put forth some strong arguments:

First . . . we are taxed in common and equally with other citizens . . . .

Second, we ask it because our ancestors were among the pioneers of our country, and we are native born citizens . . . .

Third . . . we are now making as rapid improvements in moral, intellectual and political science as any other portion of the laboring class in the state by maintaining churches, schools, temperance and beneficial societies . . . .

Fourth . . . it is a right granted to foreigners from two to five years, and whose situations and prejudices in favor of the land of their nativity do not permit them to be as well-acquainted with republican institutions as we, the native born citizens of this state.

Fifth . . . it is contrary to the genius and prosperity of any republican country to oppress her own home-born sons . . . .

The petition was rejected, but Rock continued to be a tireless advocate for his people. A year later, in remarks addressed to the state legislature, he built on the themes expressed in the petition. "We confess there is something about this we never could understand," he said. "We are denied our rights as men, [but] at the same time are taxed in common with yourselves and obliged to support the government in her denunciations [of us]. If we are not men, why are we dealt with as such when we do not pay our taxes, or when we infringe the laws? Whenever we become delinquent in the one, or a transgressor in the other, there is then no question of our manhood . . . ."

Rock was a man of many talents. In 1849, he completed his studies in dentistry. Then he enrolled in the American Medical College of Philadelphia and graduated three years later as a medical doctor. After fighting for the rights of free blacks in New Jersey, Rock moved to Boston, where he practiced as a dentist and a doctor. Just before the Civil War, he enrolled in law school, and in 1861 he was admitted to the bar in Massachusetts.

Perhaps the capstone of his life came in 1865, as the Civil War ended. He became the first black man accredited to argue cases before the United States Supreme Court.

No one should have been surprised at the achievements of Rock, a black man. For as long as anyone could remember, many free black men and some women had become skilled artisans, efficient farmers, and owners of small businesses. For example, Lizzie Nickens owned a store in Claysville, and Thomas Marshall was a shopkeeper in Marlboro.

Although many white families in Salem had opposed slavery and had themselves petitioned the state legislature, the black residents had their own learned spokespersons, men like John Rock.

Later in the century, it would be another Salem County black man, the Reverend Jeremiah H. Pierce, who would successfully argue before the state supreme court that segregated public schools were unconstitutional.

Black historian Clement Alexander Price has called Mr. Pierce's victory "one of the most important civil rights gains in the state's history." Unfortunately, the court's decision was not enforced vigorously, if at all, in many parts of the state, particularly in

George Abbott's Tide Mill Farm in
Mannington Township was a station
on the underground railroad prior to
the Civil War. Runaway slaves were
hidden in a cellar room that could only
be reached through a trap door under
vegetable bins off the kitchen. Edward
Abbott, Jr., is shown here descending a
ladder into the room, which, at the time
it was used to hide runaway slaves, included a cot, chair, table, and candle-
stick. The late Ruth Abbott Rogers, who
wrote a history of the Abbott family,
described how the cellar room was used:
"When a runaway slave managed the
three-mile stretch of the Delaware
River, pushing a log before him, and
crawled up into the salt meadows at
night . . . towards one of the great farms
rearing large on the rich meadows, he
was not turned away."
Photograph by the Bridgeton
Evening News

South Jersey. Indeed, schools in Salem were not
desegregated until after World War II.

"Choose ye this day whom ye will serve" was
the title of an editorial published in the *National
Standard & Salem County Advertiser* on Wednesday,
April 17, 1861, five days after soldiers of the
Confederate States of America had fired upon soldiers
of the United States of America at Fort Sumter,
South Carolina. "There is from this hour no longer
any middle or neutral ground to occupy," said the
editorial. "All party lines cease. Democrats,
Whigs . . . Republicans . . . all merge into one of two
parties—Patriots or Traitors."

The same day the editorial appeared, a large
crowd, perhaps moved by the fiery rhetoric in the
newspaper, gathered at the Salem County court-
house. One result was the raising of $1,000 to help
support the formation of a Salem County company of
volunteers. They left for Trenton eight days later
under the command of Robert C. Johnson, the son
of—you guessed it—the same Colonel Johnson who,
fortunately, made the people of Salem County like
tomatoes.

A month later, in May, the county Board of
Freeholders passed one resolution to appropriate an
additional $1,000 for the Johnson Guards and a
second to authorize reimbursing Samuel Plummer,
Benjamin Acton, and Jonathan Ingham for their
expenses incurred helping to outfit the soldiers sent
off to Trenton and, ultimately, to the Union's Army of
the Potomac.

Before the war was over, the freeholders had
raised through taxation more than $500,000 to
support volunteers from the county. And every
federal demand for enlistments was met by men of
the county.

One of the better known volunteers from Salem
was not a soldier, but a nurse, Cornelia Hancock of
Lower Alloways Creek. She served during the last
two years of the war, and her work was described in
glowing terms by a reporter for the *New York
Tribune*.

The post-Civil War years were boom times in
Salem County. And what helped the farmer prosper
and helped launch a new industry was the tomato.

The new industry was food processing—the
cannery or can house. The first cannery was the
Patterson and Jones Canning Factory, which began
operations in Salem in 1864. By the end of the war,
the company was turning out six hundred thousand

cans of tomatoes. Thereafter, canneries popped up around the county almost as fast and plentiful as weeds in the summer heat.

Fogg & Hires had three plants in Pennsville, Quinton, and Hancock's Bridge, and they slapped on their cans of tomatoes labels that bragged "Salem Beauty" and "Defy the World." Watson & Atkins packaged "Aldine Beauties." There were so many canneries no one could really count them. "You'd be surprised how many little canneries there were," Hamilton G. Pedrick, Jr. remembered when he was interviewed in the summer of 1983. Pedrick had worked in an Alloway cannery. "Some of them were run by women."

Some of the canneries packaged pears, peaches, pumpkins and such, but the tomato was the undisputed king (or queen). And when most of the small canneries dropped out of the picture in the late 1800s and into the twentieth century, the big corporations with worldwide markets came along to replace them: Campbell Soups in Camden, Del Monte in Swedesboro, Heinz in Salem, Hunts and Ritter in Bridgeton. The farmers could hardly grow enough tomatoes fast enough. By 1929, Salem ranked second among New Jersey's twenty-one counties in production of tomatoes.

And for the next forty years it continued to rank first or second! Thank you, Colonel Johnson.

The growing and processing of the tomato was such a grandly successful business in the county, that some sage predicted in the late 1800s, "The time is not far distant when the cultivation of wheat and other standard crops will be mostly abandoned, and the county become almost one entire market garden . . . ."

The prediction did come true—for a long while. Then, as will be noted in Chapter Six, the processors (canneries) discovered California.

Fort Delaware on Pea Patch Island offshore from Salem County in the Delaware River was a prison for captured Confederate soldiers during the Civil War. Many of the prisoners died on the island. It was not practical to bury them there, so almost 2,500 Confederate dead were interred in Salem County. After the war, some of the bodies were removed by relatives to family gravesites in the South. However, a number remained behind. Today, they lie at rest in Finns Point National Cemetery in Pennsville, along with 131 Union soldiers, dead from the Spanish-American War and World War I, and 13 German POWs who died in a camp located on the grounds of Parvin State Park. In these pictures, Company K of the Twelfth New Jersey Volunteers, a Civil War re-enactment unit, fire a volley at a memorial service held May 22, 1988.
Photographs by Stephan Harrison

A sergeant in the Twelfth Virginia Cavalry, a Civil War re-enactment unit, bows his head as taps are played during the 1988 memorial service at Finns Point National Cemetery. In the background is the monument listing the names of the honored dead.
Photograph by Stephan Harrison

Col. Robert C. Johnson, who had led the first group of volunteers from Salem County at the outbreak of the Civil War, was discharged because of a disability on February 27, 1863. For his last four months of service, Johnson was paid $743.55.
Document from the Salem County Historical Society collection

The time is Memorial Day, 1909; it has been forty-four years since the end of the Civil War. The surviving members of the Thomas A. Smythe Post of the Grand Army of the Republic have gathered again in Elmer. The veterans, from left to right, are: James P. Beckett, Lewis Wentz, John Shull, Robert Summerill, Phillip Hellina, William Overs, Emerson Sherwood, John Bates, Henry S. Paulding, Charles Cole, George Smith, Robert Wallen, John Atkinson, William Campbell, Casper Pfeffer, Frank Dunham, George W. Green, Martin Schnetzler, Jacob Frazer, and George Robinson. The boy "mascot" is Charles Harvey.
Picture from the Elmer Times collection

Henry Abbott, known to family and friends alike as Uncle Henry, was born in 1846, the eldest son of the George Abbott who built Tide Mill Farm in Mannington Township (which returned to the Abbott family in 1986 after being owned by others for a number of years). A strict Quaker, Uncle Henry always wore black, including the tall panama hat he is wearing in this picture. He varnished the hat each spring. The child he is holding, Dorothy Abbott, married and was living in Arlington, Virginia, in the summer of 1988. Uncle Henry was well-known and loved in Salem, particularly by the children. On many occasions, he would stand outside the school on Market Street and give to boys and girls homemade tops and other wooden toys. He was a recognized and respected character in Philadelphia, where he worked as a chemist. When Uncle Henry road through town on his unicycle, he was cordially greeted by Philadelphia Quakers: "Howdy do, Uncle Henry! How are thee?" He died in 1926, and his descendants lament that his famous panama hat did not survive him.

Photograph from the Edward and Elizabeth Abbott collection

For more than three centuries, ships—first under sail and then under steam—have brought people and goods in and out of Salem County, primarily at docks in the city of Salem and Penns Grove. The first picture is an overview of the Salem port as it looked in the late 1800s and early 1900s. The picture was taken from the tower of the American Oil Cloth factory that once stood on the south side of West Broadway. The Gayner Glass Works, which also has been gone for a number of years, is in the foreground. Pictures two and three show the steamboats Ulrica and Clifton at Penns Grove, and picture four is a poster the Boon Brothers & Company of Salem used in the 1830s and later to promote trips on their ship, the Clifton. If one compares the sketch showing how the Clifton actually looked with the poster, one would have to conclude that the Boons were guilty of grossly false advertising. (Notice, for example, that the poster has added three smokestacks). *Photographs from the* Today's Sunbeam *collection*

The Major Reybold, *owned by John Reybold & Brothers, was built in 1853 at Wilmington, Delaware, by Harland & Hollingsworth. The ship traveled regularly between Philadelphia, Penns Grove, and Salem (pictures five and six show the ship in Penns Grove). During the Civil War, particularly after the battle at Gettysburg, the* Major Reybold *transported Confederate prisoners to Fort Delaware on Pea Patch Island from Philadelphia. On one occasion, as the ship was pulling away from the island and heading down river, a Union gunboat fired several shots across its bow and made it turn back. Prison officials said they were missing a Confederate colonel and thought he might be a stowaway on the* Major Reybold. *An inspection of the ship did not produce the colonel, and prison officials finally concluded that he must have escaped in Philadelphia.*
Photographs and sketch from the Salem County Historical Society collection

54

The Craven *(picture one)* and the City of Salem *were two of the steamboats that plied the waters between Philadelphia and Salem County ports in the 1800s and early 1900s. Although both of these ships were built elsewhere, some small steamboats and masted schooners were built here in the county—in Alloway, of all unlikely places. If you were to visit Alloway today, you would find very little evidence of the shipbuilding industry that flourished there for four or five decades, beginning in about 1830. The firm of Reeve & Brothers built perhaps as many as thirty ships during the period (the large, fine homes owned by the Reeve family still stand along North Greenwich Street). J. H. C. Appelgate, writing in 1897 about shipbuilding in Alloway, stated, "It would require a wondrous stretch of the imagination on the part of anyone who never witnessed a vessel launch in Allowaystown to have them take in what many residents of the place have seen many times over—quite large ships launched in that miserable little stream . . . ." To launch a ship successfully, the high tide first had to*

"back up" the water in the stream. Then, the floodgates would be opened in a mill pond above the shipyard. The combined flow of water usually got the ship going, but it often required men with poles to maneuver the ship downstream to where the creek was wider

and deeper.
Photograph one from the Salem County Historical Society collection; photograph two from the Today's Sunbeam collection

Commercial canning of fruits and vegetables became widespread in the county in the decade after the Civil War. Some canneries were very small family operations and some employed several dozen persons. The canneries went by such names as these: Patterson & Lloyd, Davis & Lippincott, John S. Ewell, John Wallace, Elmer Griscom, Salem Canning Company, Chew & Bilderback, Samuel L. Kelty, Aldine Canning Factory, and Fogg & Hires. Larger companies, such as Fogg & Hires, had plants in several locations. The plant in Pennsville was located at the end of Main Street along the river. In picture one, taken in the early 1900s, wagons loaded with tomatoes are waiting to be processed at that Pennsville cannery or can house. Men are shown filling cans in the second

picture. When it came to canning whole tomatoes, the peelers, usually women who were paid three or four cents per bucket, did their work after the tomatoes had been dipped in boiling water. Men, women, and children were employed in the Fogg & Hires cannery in Hancock's Bridge (picture three). Tomatoes, of course, became the major product for commercial canning. However, peaches, pears, and pumpkins also were canned commercially, especially in the early days of the industry. A pile of pumpkins is awaiting processing at the Hancock's Bridge plant in picture four. Photographs one and two from the Harvey R. Woodlin collection; photographs three and four from the Lower Alloways Creek collection of William J. S. Bradway photographs

Three canneries were located in Quinton: Fogg & Hires, Kelty, and Ayars. Fogg & Hires and Ayars canned tomatoes exclusively, but Kelty also processed pumpkins and pears. Early in the 1900s, Fogg & Hires built the rowhouses shown here primarily for the Italian immigrants who came to work in the can house along the south bank of Alloways Creek.
Photograph by Stephan Harrison

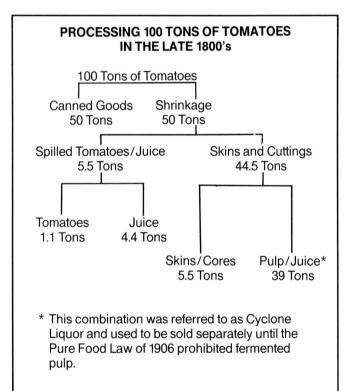

According to a January 1888 edition of the Salem Standard and Jerseyman, *this is what a farmer growing tomatoes could expect to spend and make for every five acres of tomatoes he raised.*

RAISING FIVE ACRES OF TOMATOES IN 1888

Expenses

Seed	$ 2.00
Plowing	6.00
Setting out plants	10.25
Cultivating four times	6.25
One ton phosphate	30.00
Applying phosphate	1.50
Picking 50 tons of tomatoes @ two cents per basket	60.00
Delivering 50 tons of tomatoes	50.00

Income

Selling 50 tons of tomatoes @ $6	$300.00

Profit $134.00

PROCESSING 100 TONS OF TOMATOES IN THE LATE 1800's

100 Tons of Tomatoes

Canned Goods 50 Tons — Shrinkage 50 Tons

Spilled Tomatoes/Juice 5.5 Tons — Skins and Cuttings 44.5 Tons

Tomatoes 1.1 Tons — Juice 4.4 Tons

Skins/Cores 5.5 Tons — Pulp/Juice* 39 Tons

* This combination was referred to as Cyclone Liquor and used to be sold separately until the Pure Food Law of 1906 prohibited fermented pulp.

F. E. Daniels, a chemist, compiled a table in the late 1800s that illustrated the waste and by-products when one hundred tons of tomatoes were processed by a typical cannery of the day. The development of better methods and equipment in the 1900s made the processing more efficient and profitable. However, it wasn't until the 1920s that the canneries began canning tomato juice.
From the book History of Commercial Canning in New Jersey *by Mary B. Sim; New Jersey Agricultural Society; Trenton, N.J., 1951*

The aerial view of the Salem waterfront shows the H. J. Heinz processing plant in the foreground and the Anchor-Hocking Glass plant in the background. Both operations were thriving up until the mid 1970s. While the Anchor Glass Container Corporation continues to run the glass works, the sprawling Heinz plant, also shown in the other picture, shut down in 1977. The flight of food processing plants from the county has caused most farmers to shift away from growing fruits and vegetables.

Photographs from the Today's Sunbeam *collection*

Potatoes were an important cash crop in Salem County in the late 1800s and early 1900s, particularly in the eastern half of the county. In the first picture, a farmhand cultivates a field of potatoes. The next picture shows potatoes being dug and placed in baskets. When the potatoes have been harvested, they are ready for transportation to the markets. The third picture shows the wagons loaded with potatoes lined up on Main Street in Elmer waiting for the freight cars.
Photographs from the Elmer Times *collection*

Most of the fruit grown in this part of the state now comes from apple and peach orchards in Gloucester County. However, when these pictures were taken at the Woodstown train station around 1905, apples were a cash crop in Salem County. The men are shown packing the apples in baskets and then transferring them to freight cars. The train will take the apples to markets in Philadelphia and beyond.
Photographs from the Today's Sunbeam *collection*

Farming has always meant long hours, hard work, and an uncertain reward for all the effort. However, technology has helped some. For example, the Townsend family of Alloway, shown with their horse and plow at the end of the nineteenth century, would surely have found it easier to turn over the ground with today's tractor (picture two). And the man cutting his hay in picture three would certainly marvel at the machinery that now bales the hay and sends it up a conveyor belt to be stacked on a wagon pulled behind a tractor (picture four). Imagine if the

farmers who made the land prosper in the eighteenth and nineteenth centuries would return to a farm of the late twentieth century and see insects and crop diseases controlled by chemicals that are quickly and efficiently applied (picture five); and wouldn't they be amazed to see acres of potatoes in Pittsgrove Township watered by a center pivot irrigation system, resembling a giant praying mantis and stretching almost to the horizon.

Photographs one and three from the Robert P. Dorrell collection; the other photographs by Stephan Harrison

"The time is not far distant when the other standard [field] crops will be mostly abandoned and the county become almost one entire garden and fruit farm." So wrote Irene Hancock in 1964 in a publication of the Salem County Historical Society. Fourteen years later, a county farmer said, "Vegetables for the most part are just a loss. I really think there's more of a future in grains." The farmer was right. While some vegetables and fruits are still grown, including potatoes (but no longer transported in horse-drawn wagons as shown in this picture from the early 1900s), most farmers have turned to the grains. One of the vegetables once grown in large quantities in South Jersey was asparagus, but few asparagus fields exist today. Hill's Produce and Farms in Canton is one of the last processors anywhere to still bunch asparagus for the commercial market, according to the owner, Calvin Hill. Pictures two and three show the cutting and bunching operations performed by Dan McCormick of Salem and two women from Canton, Arlene Smith (at left) and Ruth Carr. McCormick then gathers up the bunches and crates them for shipment to Philadelphia. Hill moves about two thousand crates in a season now. Photograph from the Elmer Times collection; other photographs by Stephan Harrison

This is a story of three cannons and how they got to Salem County from Italy. The cannons were cast in 1763 by a foundry in Naples and later passed into the hands of the Austrian Army. They were captured by the army of Napoleon Bonaparte when he defeated the Austrians in 1800. The French in turn lost the cannons to the British during a battle in Spain in 1808. The British took the cannons back to England and had them remade in the British image, which meant substituting a bronze barrel. The British took the cannons with them when they went to fight the Americans again during the War of 1812. The American army captured the guns at the battle of Plattsburgh, New York. After every war there is army surplus, and the three cannons qualified as such. They were sold to Salem County for $3,000. Some say the cannons were to beef up the county's arsenals. In any case, they eventually wound up in three locations: in front of the county court house in Salem (picture one), on the green that still exists at the intersection of North Main Street and Marlton Road in Woodstown (picture two, taken at the July 4, 1901 dedication), and in front of Pole Tavern, which was located near what is today the intersection of Routes 40 and 77 in Upper Pittsgrove Township (picture three, with Pole Tavern at the right). Photograph one from the Salem County Historical Society collection, photograph two from the Sam H. Jones collection, and photograph three from the Robert P. Dorrell collection

The cannons bear this crest on their barrel, which is said to represent the union of the two Spanish kingdoms of Leon and Castile.
Photograph from the Salem County Historical Society collection

The cannon that stood in front of Pole Tavern and later the Upper Pittsgrove Township Hall gradually deteriorated, and the wood on it rotted away. Early in 1986, Jay Williams and David Harvey of Daretown restored the cannon, using mostly their own money and labor. All the new wood is oak. The cannon was completed in time for the July 4 parade in Woodstown. Since then, the two men built an ammunition wagon bearing the inscription "Grand Armee de L'empereur." The cannon was featured again in the 1988 Woodstown parade, and at its conclusion the cannon was fired at the Woodstown-Pilesgrove Township recreation field on Marlton Road. Jay Williams stands at left in picture one. The other men, members of Civil War re-enactment units, are Jack Meyers of Bridgeton; Chris Meyers, his son; and Jim Fogg of Salem. Jack Meyers also is shown lighting the cannon's fuse. The cannon that stood in Woodstown disappeared forty to fifty years ago; the one in Salem still stands, and this cannon was being stored by Williams until a more suitable location can be found.
Photographs by Stephan Harrison

These are Salem street scenes in the late 1800s and early 1900s. The first picture shows the corner of market Street and Broadway, and the second picture is of the old Salem Glass Works. A large crowd at Bee's Park listens to the melodies of a band (picture three) while they wait for the main attraction, a speech by William Jennings Bryan. The Friends Meeting House in picture four was built in 1772; you can tell because, like many buildings of the period, the date has been set into the brick. The final picture shows the jail that was built in 1775 and once stood at the corner of Market Street and East Broadway.
Pictures from the Salem County Historical Society collection

It's carnival time in Salem! The date for these particular goings-on is October 6, 1909, and the carnival was sponsored by the Salem Businessmen's Association.
Photographs from the Salem County Historical Society collection

Today's veterinarians probably do not use Kendall's Spavin Cure on horses any longer, but blacksmiths like this man in the late 1800s in Woodstown, are still in demand by horse owners. Photograph from the Sam. H. Jones collection

The eight hundred-pound hog, one of the largest ever produced in the county, is being readied for slaughter, probably at the Dunham Packing Company in Alloway. The slaughterhouse was begun just before the start of the Civil War by John B. Dunham, although these pictures were taken early in the 1900s. The other picture shows one of the company's stock wagons, used to transport animals.
Photographs from the Robert P. Dorrell collection

The Willow Grove Mill near Elmer was built in 1789 and purchased nearly one hundred years later by Thomas C. Fox, who is shown here (left foreground) standing in front of the old building (he is on the right). An employee, Steve Crane, is at his side. Mill workers can be seen hanging out the second floor windows. The picture was taken in 1909; the mill burned to the ground forty years later.
Photograph from the Elmer Times *collection*

Beginning in the mid-1800s, privately owned and operated toll roads, called turnpikes, were common. Here, Albert Davis, an employee of the Salem & Bridgeton Turnpike Company, is prepared to take tolls from travelers on the Salem-Bridgeton Road (now Route 49). The turnpike companies kept the major dirt highways relatively smooth and free of rocks. As a result, most travelers were willing to pay the toll, which was a penny per mile for one horse and two cents per mile for a wagon and two horses. The gatekeeper could waive the toll under certain circumstances: if the road was in bad shape, if the traveler was taking grain to be ground for his/ her family, and for persons going to church or a funeral. The Salem & Bridgeton Turnpike Company was organized shortly after the Civil War by George M. Ward, Robert English, George Hires, Johnson Hitchner, William Shimp, Job Ayres, and John Lambert. It continued to operate until 1915.
Photograph from the Today's Sunbeam *collection*

In the late 1800s, Czar Alexander III of Russia set out on a campaign of repression against Jews in his country. As a consequence, hundreds of thousands of Jewish families fled Russia, some going to Palestine, some to other countries in Europe, but many setting sail for America. Among those who came to America were adherents of an organization called AM Olam, which intended to establish agricultural colonies in the United States. With the help of an international organization called Alliance Israelite Universelle,

based in Paris, and other groups, forty thousand followers of AM Olam emigrated to America during 1882. The first forty-three families, who came from Odessa and Kiev and other towns, reached New York in May. Some of their number scouted the countryside beyond the city and finally decided to locate in southern New Jersey at a stop on the railroad about one hundred miles from New York and fifty miles from Philadelphia. The railroad stop was then called Bradway Station; today it is the town of Norma. The Baron de

Hirsch Fund purchased land for the families, but when they arrived, they had no housing. At first they stayed in army tents supplied by the government, but by the end of the year they were living communally in this barracks, which they called Castle Garden. The families were collectively known as the Alliance Colony, the first Jewish agricultural settlement in the United States.
Photograph from the Alliance Colony Foundation collection

The land for the Alliance Colony was subdivided into fifteen-acre parcels. Each parcel was numbered on a map, and the head of each of the forty-three families picked a number out of a hat to learn which parcel belonged to him. The land did not exactly belong to the farmers, however. Since they had no money, their land, two-room house (one upstairs and one down), and well were mortgaged to the Alliance Land Trust established by the Baron De Hirsch Fund. One of the original synagogues built by the colonists was B'nai Anshei Estreich in Brotmanville. The building still exists, but the restored pulpit and other religious paraphernalia have been moved to a small museum operated by the Alliance Colony Foundation on Gershal Avenue in Norma (picture one). The colonists, none of whom had been farmers in Russia, received much help from Christian farmers in the area. During the remaining years of the nineteenth century, more families arrived, and the colony grew. A Chevra Kadisha (cemetery association) was formed (see its constitution), and by 1900 the Jewish Agricultural Association had made arrangements for a Unitarian educator and his family to visit the colony monthly and bring culture and learning; Prof. Louis J. G. B. Mounier (picture three) lectured on history and current events, his wife played piano, and his daughter sang.

Photograph one by Stephan Harrison; other photographs from the Alliance Colony Foundation collection

These are members of families that were a part of the Alliance Colony in the late 1800s and early 1900s. The first picture shows Martha and Raphael Crystal, who arrived in the colony from Odessa in 1890. Other members of the Crystal family, Rachel and Jacob, are shown in 1915 standing beside a barnstorming plane that landed in a nearby field (picture two). The young Crystals paid one dollar to get their picture taken; it was another two dollars to go up in the plane. Joseph Greenblatt is seen in 1910 with his horse, Nellie, at his first home, located at the corner of Gershal and Steinfeldt avenues in Brotmanville (picture three). In picture four, Jacob Greenblatt is delivering leghorn chickens to the Vineland railroad station for transpor-

tation to the market in Philadelphia. Finally, a second generation colonist is shown in his World War I uniform on a plow probably used on his family's farm. Many of the later colonists did not take up farming, but were employed in small plants that sprung up to make clothing for New York firms. Among the persons born in the Alliance Colony was Joseph B. Perskie, who was the first Jew appointed to the New Jersey Supreme Court. Also born in Alliance was Frank A. Golder, who became an advisor to Presidents Wilson and Hoover. Herbert Kraft, whose family were colonists, built the Roxy Theater in New York.

Photographs from the Alliance Colony Foundation collection

Could it actually be a woman driver in 1910? Of course, and in the latest Franklin car. The picture was taken along the Alloway-Aldine Road. No record exists to tell us who this foursome is, but the flags would indicate that the occasion for this jaunt in the country might have been a holiday. By the way, both men are wearing goggles. The man in the front seat has his pushed up on his cap, while the man in the back seat has his down over his eyes. Photograph from the Sam H. Jones collection

They Who Worked In New Industries

On a very warm July day in 1891, the brothers duPont—Alexis, Alfred, Charles, Eugene, Francis, and Henry—were deeded approximately two hundred acres of the old Carney tract south of Penns Groves. The land bulged out slightly from the shoreline into the Delaware River and was known as Carney's Point.

What the duPonts started there was known as the Carney's Point Works. The plant helped the allies win two world wars, and the Du Pont Chambers Works down river at Deepwater Point helped change the way people live in Philadelphia, London, Moscow, Tokyo, and nearly everywhere else.

Not incidentally, the two plants also changed the history of Salem County.

The Carney's Point Works began by making smokeless gunpowder, mostly for shotguns. Powder for rifles and cannons was manufactured in large quantities during the Spanish-American War. By the summer of 1904 the number of employees had grown from fifteen or so men to nearly forty, and county residents thought the expansion was something of a boom.

But they had not seen anything yet!

Thirteen summers later the Carney's Point Works had more then twenty-five thousand men and women working around the clock turning out gunpowder for the armies of the United States, Great Britain, France, Italy, Russia, and the other allies battling the forces of the Kaiser. Since most of the workers had families, the actual number of persons who poured into the county in a matter of months has been estimated at nearly one hundred thousand.

Many of the new workers were recruited from among the approximately nine million European immigrants who entered this country from 1901 to 1910.

The county, particularly the communities immediately surrounding Carney's Point, tried to adapt to the influx. It wasn't easy. The Penns Grove school system, which enrolled three hundred students, saw five thousand children show up in one week during World War I. Every available space in the area was turned into a classroom.

A barracks community was created where the Sakima Country Club and Salem Community College are now located, and the company built whole villages of small bungalows and two-story houses. Still another community sprouted—what one Du Pont official refers to as Orange Crate City. The "city" consisted mostly of tents, shacks, little hotels and stores, and moonshiners' stills, according to Robert Shinn of Pennsville. Mr. Shinn is engineering manager of the Du Pont corporation, former manger of the Chambers Works, and unofficial historian for the Du Pont plants in the county.

The typical schedule for this vast army of

workers, a number of whom could not speak English, was twelve days on the job and one day off. Shinn said some enterprising homeowners in the area rented the same quarters to more than one person or family. While one set of roomers was at work, the others slept.

"The whole experience was a phenomenon that outstrips the gold rush and anything else," said Shinn.

Of the tens of thousands of workers recruited for the Carney's Point plant, many settled in the county with their families after the war.

Loyal and long family ties to Du Pont are legendary. Forty relatives of Mr. and Mrs. Shinn have worked at the county's two Du Pont facilities. Shinn's grandfather was one of the early employees at Carney's Point, leaving his Auburn farm for the factory and better pay in 1894. Shinn's father, who was ninety-eight in the summer of 1988, worked all his life for Du Pont, beginning in 1911. If his father had purchased Du Pont stock when he first had the opportunity, Shinn said, it would be "worth millions today."

Both of Mrs. Shinn's grandfathers, Luigi Traini and Giuseppe Maconi, came from Italy in the decade preceding World War I. Grandfather Traini came to work for Du Pont because an older brother, who had arrived in this country earlier, was employed at a plant in Gibbstown (Gloucester County).

Shortly before the outbreak of the war, he returned briefly to Italy, then came back to work at the Chambers Works as a laborer. When he retired from Du Pont, he was employed in the power plant.

Mrs. Shinn's father was one of eleven children; all of them worked for Du Pont.

Shinn estimates that 38 percent of the county's total population are either current Du Pont em-

ployees, Du Pont pensioners, or members of their immediate family.

What happened at the Carney's Point plant during World War I pretty much overshadowed concurrent developments a few miles away at Deepwater Point. But those developments were destined to be of far greater significance to the nation and the world.

It was the summer of 1917, with the Carney's Point

When Du Pont began operations at Carney's Point in the late 1800s, the plant was—well—unimpressive, as this view from 1894 illustrates (picture one). In the early years, water for the plant was supplied by Thomas Carney's old grist mill (picture two). Cotton was used to make nitrated cellulose, the basic ingredient in smokeless gunpowder, and the cotton came to the Carney's Point plant mainly in six hundred or nine hundred bales of cuttings from factories that made cotton shirts or other materials. In the late 1800s, the cotton bales were moved on flatcars pulled by mules (picture three). Picture four shows the old ballistic

plant operating at full capacity, when E. I. duPont de Nemours & Company announced its decision "to enter the coal tar dye industry." Prior to World War I, Germany had a lock on the dye industry, and by 1917 the world market was practically devoid of dyes needed for everything from postage stamps to the uniforms our doughboys were wearing in France.

Earlier in the war years, Dr. A. D. Chambers, a Du Pont chemist, had come east from Colorado to help the company develop new sources of toluene, an important ingredient in explosives.

In a memorandum dated July 26, 1915, Dr. Chambers noted that some of the compounds used in the making of explosives were the same or similar to those used in the manufacture of dyes.

range where the smokeless power was tested. The Sporting Powder gang seen in picture five were men who helped make the powder for shotguns and other weapons used by sportsmen in 1911, when this picture was made. The men, from left, are William Van Culin, Webster Davis, Joseph Stiles, George Luker, Harvey McCarson, and Filbert Sparks—their foreman. Inside the wagon and hardly visible in the picture are William Megill and James Hutchinson.
Photographs reprinted from special 1951 and 1952 anniversary issues of The Carney's Pointer

81

Eventually, some twenty-five hundred dyes were manufactured at the Chambers Works (Shinn's father helped mix the first batch). But the dye business was only the beginning. It led to a tremendous expansion of Du Pont's organic chemicals division, and today the company manufactures at the Chambers Works plant more then one thousand compounds that are used to make many of the products found in houses around the globe (and as part of the houses themselves).

"In the civilized world," said Shinn, " it would be hard to stand more than 100 feet away from a product that could not be traced to the Chambers Works plant." Carney's Point operations ceased in the late 1970s.

In the years after the Civil War, another important industry in the county was spawned. The American Oil Cloth Company began making a new kind of floor covering in its Salem plant in 1868. This company was succeeded by a branch of the Congoleum Company. But it is John B. Campbell and his family who have exercised the greatest impact on the floor covering industry and on the Salem County economy.

Campbell organized the Salem Linoleum Works in 1913, which later became the Mannington Mills. The company, with its roots planted firmly in the county, chose for its logo a silhouette of the great Lenape Indian chief, Maneto.

Although the company now has four subsidiaries with a worldwide market, it is still owned by the Campbell family. The corporate headquarters and the principal plant manufacturing floor covering are located in Mannington Township along Fenwick Creek. The facilities in the county employ more then seven hundred persons.

Historian Joseph S. Sickler credits the new industries with attracting to Salem County "a solid and growing population of worthwhile people." Writing in the 1930s, Sickler went on to say that this "new blood" and these new industries, along with the radio and automobile, had forever broken the "county's rural isolation and provincialism."

The men of "new blood" and "old blood" together shed their red blood during World War II, and their names are honored on the county's memorial tablets. For example: Charles Agnew, Carman Brigandi, Percy Campbell, Anthony Checchia, Meredith Draper, Joseph Dimatteo, John Jordan, Adam Kacewich, and on and on. ∎

These are shop workers at Du Pont in the first decade of the twentieth century (pictures one and two). Notice how young the man, or boy, working with a screwdriver appears to be. With the outbreak of World War I, Du Pont and Salem County were changed forever. The panorama shows a portion of Carney's Point Village (picture three), located just south of Penns Grove, which was constructed by Du Pont during the war boom. Many of the homes are still standing, but the barracks in the background were torn down shortly after the war. When the United States entered the war in 1917, Du Pont began to lose men to the army. On August 20 of that year a small shack was put up outside the gate of the main entrance where a small number of women could be recruited for "light

work" that required a "keen eye." Ten days later, twenty-five local girls had signed on; by the end of December the plant was employing 1,965 women from all over the country. The single women were housed in dormitories. The company called the women "Powder Girls," but because of the uniform they were required to wear, they also were called "Bloomer Girls" (picture four). Most of the women employed during World War I left at war's end to make room for the returning veterans and to start families. However, twenty-four years later Du Pont again had to put out the call for women workers, and again they responded in large numbers (picture five).

Photographs reprinted from special 1951 and 1952 anniversary issues of The Carney's Pointer

This is the picric acid nitrating and wash house at Carney's Point where Du Pont made its first batch of dye in 1916. Dye manufacturing later was moved to Deepwater Point and became the nucleus of Du Pont's mammoth organic chemicals industry.
Photograph from the Robert Shinn collection

Charles Pedersen of Salem (sitting), born in 1904 of a Japanese mother and Norwegian father, won the Nobel Prize for chemistry in 1987. He was honored for his nine years of research on polymers and ethers at Du Pont's Chambers Work plant. Pedersen is shown here looking at a portrait of him and fellow scientists at the Jackson Labs. Colleagues looking over his shoulder are, from the left, Kalman Marcali, Erik Kissa, and Maimus Yllo. The man in the background is not identified.
Photograph from the Today's Sunbeam *collection*

Many glassmakers took off from where Richard Wistar left off in the late 1700s. Among them was the Salem Glass Works, which began operations in 1895 at a plant on Griffith Street, Salem. The company later became the Anchor Cap Company, which in turn merged with the Hocking Glass Corporation. In 1983, the glass container division of Anchor-Hocking split from the parent corporation and became the separate company known as Anchor Glass Containers Corporation. These pictures taken in the 1930s show skilled glass blowers at work and a woman packaging bottles. Today, the plant employs more than three hundred persons.

Photographs from the Today's Sunbeam *collection*

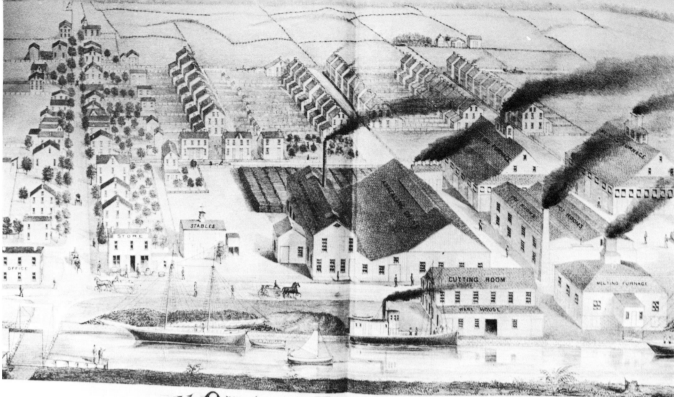

QUINTON GLASS COMPANY

This is an artist's rendering of what the old Quinton Glass Works was supposed to look like in the late 1800s. In the lower left can be seen the drawbridge over Alloways Creek. The Glass Works opened for business in 1863 and lasted for forty-six years. In its peak years, the plant employed 150 persons and annually manufactured three million feet of plate glass. Much of the glass for the Centennial Exposition buildings in Philadelphia in 1876 came from the Quinton Glass Works.
Lithograph from Sam H. Jones collection.

Sam Bassett built this glass works along the railroad tracks in Elmer in 1896. He made bottles here for a few years until his glass blowers threatened to join a union and strike. Two things Bassett wouldn't tolerate were unions and whiskey, probably in that order. He sold the plant to the Novelty Glass Company, which had bought some jar-blowing equipment from a junkman. Unfortunately, the junkman evidently had obtained the equipment illegally, and the original owner sued the Novelty Glass Company—and won. As a result, the company went out of business. Isaac Shoemaker, who had been a part owner in the Novelty Glass Company, tried to keep the plant going by manufacturing electrical supplies and glassware, but he went out of business in 1909, four years after this picture was taken. The buildings were demolished.
Photograph from the Sam H. Jones collection

In the late 1880s, when this picture was taken of employees at the Window Light Company of Elmer, a skilled glass blower earned around $135 a month. The Window Light Company opened for business in 1885, with a stock company composed of glass blowers as owners. The company, which manufactured only window glass, was the first in a succession of glass works that operated in Elmer, most of them not very successfully, into the early 1900s.
Photograph from the Elmer Times *collection*

Woodrow Wilson, when this picture was taken, was president of Princeton University and seeking to become the governor of New Jersey. Wilson ran on the Democratic ticket, pledged to reform state government and his party's political machinery. He went on to do both things. Here he is seen standing in front of the telephone pole (facing the camera) in the center of Woodstown.
Photograph from the Sam H. Jones collection, which includes many photographs taken by Edward W. Humphreys of Woodstown

Democrats in Lower Alloways Creek Township in the early 1900s (as well as now) usually did not have much to cheer about, because, it seems, the Republicans always won. However, in November 1910, Woodrow Wilson, a Democrat, was elected governor of New Jersey, and it was an occasion for boasting and raising the flag. Taking part in the ceremony are, from the left: J. P. Smick, Frank Hewitt, Mr. Sealey, Bill Hewitt, George Hewitt, John Finlaw, John Maskell, Isaac Smick (holding end of flag), and Ed Pomffer (holding end of dog).
Photograph from the B. Harold Smick, Jr. collection

Isaac Smick and his wife, Ann, and mother-in-law, Mrs. Allen, stand in front of their home in Canton in August 1912.
Photograph from the B. Harold Smick, Jr. collection

Shimp and Harris's General Store in Canton as it appeared in the first decade of the twentieth century.
Photograph from the B. Harold Smick, Jr. collection

The year is 1912, and in one picture the residents of Woodstown and vicinity have parked their vehicles at the Woodstown train station and are waiting for the arrival of President William Howard Taft's train. Republican Taft, seen speaking from the car platform in the other picture, was running for re-election against Democrat Woodrow Wilson, then governor of New Jersey. Wilson won. The train station was moved some years ago to a lot east of Woodstown on Route 40. It was still for sale in the summer of 1988.
Photographs from the Sam H. Jones collection

The Salem County Fair, a tradition for over a century, was held for many years on the auction grounds owned by the Harris family of Woodstown. Here, in 1924, people are flocking to see the Sam Lawrence Shows and, perhaps, to eat one of Huber's quality bread rolls and to guzzle a bottle of Davis's soda. Today, the auction grounds, which were along North Main Street between the Auburn Road and West Grant Street, is the site of many homes. Howard (Stoney) Harris, Jr., moved the auction and flea market, with a rodeo that had been added in 1929, to farmland west of Woodstown on Route 40, where it sill flourishes as Cowtown. Stoney Harris was introduced to auctioneering at a young age by his father, who said of his son: "I never could hire an auctioneer worth a damn, so I raised one!" Photograph from the Sam H. Jones collection

For thirty-five years, beginning in 1870, the West Jersey Agricultural and Horticultural Association operated fairgrounds on land south of today's intersection of Routes 40 and 45 in Pilesgrove Township. Part of the property is now occupied by a Wawa store. The Association sponsored farm-related exhibitions and competitions, but an important feature of the fairgrounds was this racetrack. Some of the exhibition buildings are seen in the background. The picture was taken in about 1904. After the Association closed its fairgrounds in 1905, Howard Harris, Sr., bought most of the buildings and moved them to the site of his auction and fairgrounds on North Main Street, Woodstown.
Photograph from the Sam H. Jones collection

The city of Salem also had a track for harness racing. It was located along what is now Johnson Street off South Broadway. Built in 1902, it lasted only a dozen years. Races held on Thursdays, Fridays and Saturdays often drew large crowds.
Photograph from the Salem County Historical Society collection

It is always a grand day when the circus comes to town! This covey of clowns appeared in Woodstown in the early 1900s.
Photograph from the Sam H. Jones collection

When this picture was taken in Alloway in the early 1900s, there was no tiger in Exxon because no one had to worry about super-fast acceleration. Note, of course, that the Standard Oil wagon was drawn by horses.
Photograph from the Robert P. Dorrell collection

Nathaniel Somers was a clock mender in 1903 in Woodstown when this picture was taken. He took his time, but worked diligently. He knew his craft, and he did not overcharge.
Photograph from the Sam H. Jones collection

When the old-timers say it does not snow these days like it used to when they were children, they are remembering scenes like this. Here, a horse and wagon—not a sleigh, notice—are bumping along a snow-covered Marlton Road in Pilesgrove Township on the last day of January in 1905.
Photograph from the Sam H. Jones collection

Public education always has been strong in Salem County, with relatively few children enrolled in parochial or private schools. One of the old schools is the Friendship School near Canton (picture one), where the teacher, Miss Newcomb, had no trouble giving individual attention to Mary Shourds (picture two). The Quinton School is shown in picture three, and the Good Hope one-room school in Pittsgrove Township is seen in picture four. The school had eight grades and one teacher. Photographs one and two from the B. Harold Smick, Jr. collection; photograph three from the Shirley Owens collection; and photograph four from the Paul Schmidt, Jr. collection

This is Quinton's first school bus, and the year the picture was taken is 1922. The bus is a converted market wagon, and the driver is Ben Stevenson. The children in the front row, from the left, are Morris Harris, Tommy Counsellor, Sara McQuilton, Jane Counsellor (small child), Lillian McPherson, Willard Massey, and Ellis Chesel. In the back row are Albert McPherson, Harry Lickey, Charlie Grant, and Rose Harris (obscured in the wagon). Photograph from the Shirley Owens collection

One of the most photographed persons in the late 1800s and early 1900s was Nick Turner, who delivered mail and drove the stagecoach in the southwest corner of the county. Turner greeted everyone the same way: "Hello, sporty!" During the summer, Turner grew strawberries and sold six quarts for a quarter. Photograph from the Today's Sunbeam *collection*

The date is February 25, 1904, and if you had lived at the time on one of the rural postal routes in Elmer, you would have gone out to your box along the road and picked up the mail left there by Mrs. Mahala H. Linch. Photograph from the Elmer Times *collection*

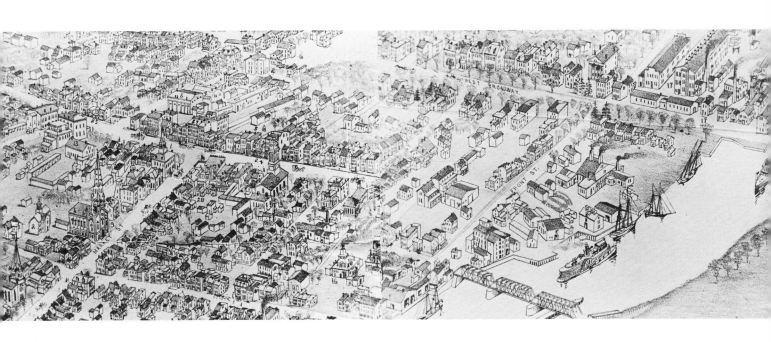

This is an artist's impression of the city of Salem in the late 1800s. In the first part of the drawing, the heart of town is shown, with the intersection of Market Street and Broadway in the center. The second part of the drawing depicts lower Broadway and the port on the Salem River. Note that the port includes both sailing ships and paddle wheel steamboats.
Drawing from the Salem County Historical Society collection

The Salem County Historical Society is called to order for the first time in 1886 in the city of Salem's Public Library. Those in attendance, from the left, are William Patterson, Thomas Shourds, William Hilliard, George Mecum, and I. Oakford Acton. Today's visitor to the library on Broadway can see the spot where the picture was taken in front of the fireplace. The same busts adorn the mantle.
Photograph from the Salem County Historical Society collection

These are street scenes in Elmer during the first decade of the twentieth century. The train arrives at the station in the first picture, and a group of ladies and children are present either to board or to greet someone getting off. The trains no longer come and go in Elmer, and the station no longer exists. In the second picture, a horse and carriage drive up Main Street from the south. The steeple of the United Methodist Church is the only landmark that would be recognizable to a person standing where the photographer stood. Ike Munyan's Butcher Shop wagon gets ready to roll in the third picture. Finally, patrons of the Elmer Lake Hotel stand on the front porch as if to bid us welcome for a couple of days or a couple of weeks in the fresh air of the country. Elmer is still surrounded by farms and still enjoys the fresh air, but the hotel no longer shelters visitors. Today, as the Lakeside Manor, it is a home for senior citizens.

Photographs from the Elmer Times *collection*

*The Elmer Borough Hall is dedicated in 1909. In the spring of 1904, $2,500 was approved by voters for construction of the municipal building, but it wasn't until February 1906 that property on Main Street was purchased for $600. Frank L. Suplee, a local contractor, was elected two years later to erect the structure, which measured thirty-six by sixty feet. The final cost of the building was more than double what had been appropriated five years earlier, which proves that nothing has changed over the years when it comes to final cost vis a vis original estimate, particularly when a government project is involved.
Photograph from the* Elmer Times *collection*

*It's a barn raising, and the time is the turn of the century—twentieth, that is. Taking part are Frank Kandle (seated center), and, standing in the first row left to right, Miss Lynch (not otherwise identified), Mrs. Hallie Lynch (presumably Miss Lynch's mother), Grandfather Dodge (with his hand on the rope), Frank Supple, and Earl Curry. The man at the far right of the first row of standees is not identified. In the back row are William Nichols, Herbert Dodge, Emerson DuBois, Mr. Birch (no first name provided), and Fletcher Smith.
Photograph from the* Elmer Times *collection*

*Isaac B. Reeves (left) and John Bishop (right) load milk from their creamery aboard a freight train in Elmer railroad station. The year is 1909.
Photograph from* Elmer Times *collection*

The Elmer Times *began publishing in this building on State Street in 1892, perhaps fifteen years before this picture was taken. In 1988, the weekly newspaper was still being published in the same building. The newspaper was founded by Samuel Preston Foster and has been in the family ever since. His great grand-daughter, Pamela Brunner, was the editor in 1988. Shown standing in front of the building (from left to right) are Malvern Reeves, S. P. Foster, Mellie Craig (in doorway), Jed Du Boise, an unidentified boy, Stanley Craig, Harry Zahn, Paul Harris, and George Lashley. Photograph from the* Elmer Times *collection.*

Al-Jo Voeckler, office manager at the Elmer Times, looks through some of the old files in the old cabinets in the century-old building where the paper is published. The portrait at the top of the picture is of Samuel Preston Foster, the founder of the paper in the late 1800s. The portrait at the right is of Preston Samuel Foster, his son, who succeeded as publisher. Preston Samuel Foster, Jr., was the publisher in 1988. Photograph by Stephan Harrison

101

This looks like a scene from a play or a recruiting poster, but it is neither. These are Spanish-American War veterans from the Elmer area who posed rather dramatically for the camera less than ten years after the short war's end. All those pictured have not been identified. However, T. Clark Murphy, at left standing, later became an Elmer policeman.
Photograph from the Elmer Times *collection*

Everyone along the east coast was digging out from the blizzard of March 1888, and part of the effort in Salem County included clearing the railroad tracks. The track clearing between Elmer and Bridgeton (Cumberland County) required two locomotives, one following the other. A third locomotive pulled two passengers cars loaded with men from the Elmer area who went to see the huge banks of snow piled up by the front engines. Suddenly, three miles below Elmer, the plow on the lead engine became stuck, bringing it almost to a standstill. The following engines were unable to brake in time, resulting in what is believed to be the worst train wreck ever in the county. The lead locomotive was thrown twelve feet off the track and turned upside down; its tender was thrown over the engine. The second engine turned over on its side (seen at right in this picture); the third locomotive, with the passengers cars, also ran off the tracks, and one of the coaches was nearly destroyed (left and foreground). Miraculously, no one was killed or gravely injured.
Photograph from the Sam H. Jones collection

102

PENNSYLVANIA RAILROAD SYSTEM.

WEST JERSEY RAILROAD.

A few freight trains still rumble through Salem County, but the railroads, which, along with steamboats, once were responsible for transporting nearly all people and goods in and out of the county, are now merely a shadow of their former selves. In the late 1800s and early 1900s many men and some women commuted to work in Camden and Philadelphia by train. As this timetable shows, the West Jersey Railroad, a division of the Pennsylvania Railroad System, had eight passenger trains going between Philadelphia and Salem daily, except Sunday. The other stops in the county were at Woodstown, Fenwick, Riddleton, Alloway, and Penton. Fenwick station was located near where the Mannington-Yorketown Road crosses the track today, and the Riddleton station was located roughly where Barber Road crosses the track in Alloway Township. Alloway Junction was near to where Route 540 crosses the track north of the present center of Alloway, and the Penton stop was in the vicinity of the intersection of Penton Station Road and Dolbow Road. All of these place names are on current Salem County road maps, and the route of the track can be followed as it enters Salem County from Gloucester County. Document reprinted from the June 1986 edition of The Way It Used to Be, *a Salem County Cultural and Heritage Commission publication*

All aboard for Bridgeton! The Salem Rapid Transit Company (probably more rapid than some public systems today) operated a coach service between Salem and Bridgeton in the early 1900s. This picture was taken about 1904, and the driver (foreground) is Walter Jordan. His passenger is not identified.
Photograph from the Today's Sunbeam *collection*

In 1918 in Pittsgrove Township, when a family wanted to build a new house, it meant excavating with a team of horses and a large scoop. Here, William Schmidt (wearing the hat and holding the reins) and his son, Paul Schmidt, Sr. (guiding the scoop), are digging the hole for a new house on Willow Grove Road. The house still stands.
Photograph from the Paul Schmidt, Jr. collection

Oh, remember the days when entertainment was neither violent nor obscene. This warning to performers was posted backstage at the Woodstown Opera House by the owner, E. W. Humphreys. The Opera House, which dates to the late 1800s, has not been used for more than twenty years and is in disrepair. However, a new owner was quoted in the spring of 1988 as saying he wanted to preserve and perhaps restore the building.
Photograph from the Sam H. Jones collection

It is Sunday morning in the first decade of the twentieth century and members of the Friendship Methodist Church in Monroeville arrive for the weekly worship service.
Photograph from the Elmer Times collection

*These are Alloway street scenes during
the first two decades of the twentieth
century. Except for vehicular traffic
today, the center of town probably was
as busy eighty and ninety years ago as
now. For one thing, the hotel, shown in
the first picture, was in operation. The
building is still there, but is no longer a
hotel. Pictures two and three are of
Greenwich Street. In picture two, the
camera is pointing north on Greenwich
Street toward the intersection of Main
Street and the Alloway-Quinton Road.
The country store operated today by the
Dorrells can be seen in the right background. Picture three looks northwest
toward Salem from the intersection
with the Alloway-Quinton Road, and
the Dorrell store is in the left foreground. The fourth picture is of a home
which still stands at the corner of Main
and Church streets.
Photographs from the Robert P. Dorrell
collection*

The story behind these pictures, taken in the early 1900s, may go something like this: A sudden storm has flooded the lanes of Alloway, and some of the ladies have been caught out shopping or calling on neighbors. In the first picture, Mrs. Jess Dorrell has been "picked up," so to speak, by her husband. The Methodist Church and cemetery in the left background indicate they are on Church Street. Evidently, the other three ladies are not quite so lucky and, for the time being, must remain high and dry on the fence. Photograph from the Robert P. Dorrell collection

It was usually a big cast when the ladies put on one of their shows at the Alloway Baptist Church. Women took all the parts, including the "men" in the front row. The time is the late teens or early twenties of this century.
Photograph from the Robert P. Dorrell collection

The year is 1913, and these folks are trying out a new potato planter in a field near Alloway. A long-time resident of the area believes the farmer at left is Frank Bell and that the two young ladies are his daughters: Mattie in the wagon and Helen in the white dress.
Photograph from the Robert P. Dorrell collection

Margaret Remster of Alloway sits with friends by her dock on Alloway Creek in the early 1900s. Nothing special is going on. Just a quiet time in a quiet place. The Remster family emigrated to Salem County from Holland in 1750.
Photograph from the Robert P. Dorrell collection

William J. S. Bradway, like any good photographer who wants to sell his work, took lots of pictures of people—at work, at play, and in more formal settings. These pictures were all taken between 1907 and 1912. His relatives, Uncle Joe and Aunt Mary Bradway, strike a pose in the first picture, and other members of the Bradway clan are shown sitting on the front porch of their home. Note that the mother and youngest son appear groomed for the picture-taking, whereas the father and two oldest boys look like they just ran in from the fields. In the third picture, the students at Harmersville School in Lower Alloways Creek line up for the camera with their teacher, Mrs. Sparks (in middle). The ladies and gentlemen in the fourth picture are not re-enacting Washington's crossing of the Delaware. Bradway describes the scene simply as a boating party. It is hoped, however, the party did not venture too far, because the boat appears to be overloaded.

Photographs from the Lower Alloways Creek collection

Fishing and crabbing usually have been good in the rivers, streams, and marshes of Salem County, but mostly people have caught fish and crabs for their own use and to sell locally. Large-scale commercial fishing and crabbing have never been among the county's major industries. Shad, a much-prized eating fish, have run up the Delaware River for many generations and continue to do so even today. These pictures from the first decade of this century show some serious and not-so-serious anglers and crabbers. Shad fishermen are

shown mending their nets in the first picture, and in the second picture the fishing boats are lined up in front of the fishermen's houses. The ladies are said to be doing a little crabbing off Cooper's Branch Bridge. They are, from left to right, Mrs. Annie Harris, Mrs. Chrissie Schrier, Miss Wick, Miss Newcomb, and Miss Hewitt—all of whom are identified as teachers. The little boy is not identified.

Photographs by William J. S. Bradway from the Lower Alloways Creek collection

The Baptist Church in Canton was, and still is, an important part of life in Lower Alloways Creek. The Reverend Elmer Hall was the minister when these pictures were taken, about 1910. During the warm weather, baptism was performed in the stream behind the church. As the person being baptized was immersed, those church members standing on the bank sang, "Shall we gather at the river." After immersion, the congregation sang, "Hallelujah! 'tis done; I believe in the Son." Photographs by William J. S. Bradway from the Lower Alloways Creek collection

Here are Alexander Bradway, the father, and William J. S. Bradway the son. The elder Bradway was a farmer and is shown here cradling wheat shortly after the turn of the century. His son, the photographer, was born in Hancock's Bridge June 7, 1861. He left succeeding generations a fine pictorial record of what rural life in Salem County was like seventy and eighty years ago.
Photographs by William J. S. Bradway from the Lower Alloways Creek collection

Happy birthday, America! It is July 4 in the first decade of the twentieth century, and Elmer is holding a parade to honor the nation's birth. F. L. Suplee, a building contractor in Centerton, has entered this float.
Photograph from the F. L. Suplee collection

Serious hunters in the county often have formed clubs, some more formal than others, and some organized to hunt one animal more than any other. For example, these are rabbit hunters from Lower Alloways Creek in the first picture. Standing, left to right, are Leonard Smick, Harry Featherer, Clifford Smick, William Smick, and Leslie Smick. Sitting are Richard B. Griscom, Alphonso Smick, and Joseph Butcher. The second picture is of a deer hunting club standing in front of the Smick Lumber Company in Quinton in December 1929. The group even had its own cook (kneeling center in chef's hat), Henry "Buck Shot Beans" Hannold. Indeed, many of the club members had nicknames. Those pictured include the five-year-old B. Harold Smick, Jr. (far left, with only his head showing), who now owns the lumber company. The men seated, from the left, are Jack Carll, Fred LaBoube, Granville "Grunt" Harris, and George "Barney" Scull. Standing in the second row are Joe Rankins, Jr.,; R. Miller Elwell; Howard Lilly; B. Harold Smick, Sr.; and Austin "Pucker" Kelty. In the rear are Smith "Mitt" Harris, Roy Horner, Charles C. Lambert, and Kenneth R. Bradway, Sr. Holding the deer heads at right are Henry "Dead Eye" Shimp, Leon Hitchner, Byron "By" Harris, Clarence Loveland, and "Doc" Emel.

Photograph one is by William J. S. Bradway from the Lower Alloways Creek collection; the second photograph is from the B. Harold Smick, Jr. collection

It started with the train and steamboat in the 1800s, then mushroomed in the first half of the 1900s with the advent of the car and improved roads. It was Salem County's becoming the place to go for recreation and fresh air if you were a couple or a family from the cities of Camden, Philadelphia, or Wilmington sweating out the summer heat and enduring the smoke and noise of urban industrialism. Folks had their pick between Delaware River beaches, with their amusements, and the many lakes in the eastern half of the county. Early stops for daily excursionists and vacationers alike were French's Hotel in Penns Grove (picture one) and Oakwood Beach in Elsinboro (pictures two and three). French's Hotel offered

swimming in the river and a lovely grove of trees to walk through or sit under (picture four). The late William B. Vanneman, writing in the Salem Standard and Jerseyman in 1969, remembered going by hay wagon to a picnic at Oakwood Beach: "...we would swoop down on the bath houses to get our suits on and into the river. If it was low tide, we would go for a wade; if it was high tide, we would go for a swim. In those days, we were satisfied with a lot less than we have today, and a picnic at Oakwood Beach was quite a treat."

Photographs one and four from the Sam H. Jones collection; photographs two and three from the Salem County Historical Society collection

The White Line ran steamboats down from Philadelphia to Riverview Beach Amusement Park in Pennsville, and they were always jammed (pictures one, two and three). Visitors could go swimming in the river or in the olympic size pool (picture four). The pool measured seventy-five by one hundred-fifty feet, held sixty thousand gallons of water, and offered bathers hot and cold showers in the bath houses. When it was built in 1936, the pool cost $150,000. For those who liked amusements, the park offered five ferris wheels and two roller coasters (picture five). Of course, there were many other rides and also places to eat. Riverview Park still exists, but gone are the swimming, the amusements and the dance hall that featured music by Henry Hedrickson's Louisville Serenaders—"Masters of Symphonic Syncopation."

Photographs from the Harvey R. Woodlin collection

Whitaker's Park on Centerton Lake was a favorite place for picnickers and vacationers. The park, which flourished in the early decades of the 1900s, was owned and operated by Lewis Whitaker, shown in the left foreground of picture one. The lake resort featured swimming and boating and a large pavilion (picture two). The park's merry-go-round (picture three) ran on water power from the saw mill on the Whitaker property.
Photographs from the F. L. Suplee collection

Gen. Gersham Mott commanded New Jersey volunteers in the Civil War. In gratitude, the federal government, when it established a shore battery at Finn's Point just before the Spanish-American War, named the installation Fort Mott. However, no Spanish armada sailed up the Delaware during that war, and neither did German ships during World War I. So, in 1922, the army abandoned the fort. It is now a state park. These pictures, taken in 1905, show the flag pole standing in front of the officers quarters and the enlisted men's barracks. Notice the soldiers standing at the top of the center barracks steps. Also, two men are standing in the shadows at the near end of the second floor porch.
Photographs from the Sam H. Jones collection

For almost ten years, beginning in 1933, the Civilian Conservation Corps was engaged throughout the country in a variety of public works projects. One of these was the construction of Parvin State Park in the southeast corner of the county in Pittsgrove Township. The young men, who lived in barracks (picture one), built Thundergust Lake, beginning with the clearing of the land (pictures two and three). A culvert also was constructed at the foot of the lake (picture four). When the men finished their work, the lake was ready to serve the recreational needs of the people of New Jersey (picture five). The corps also built cabins that are used today by campers who spend a night or a week in the park (picture six).

Photographs from the Parvin State Park Appreciation Committee collection

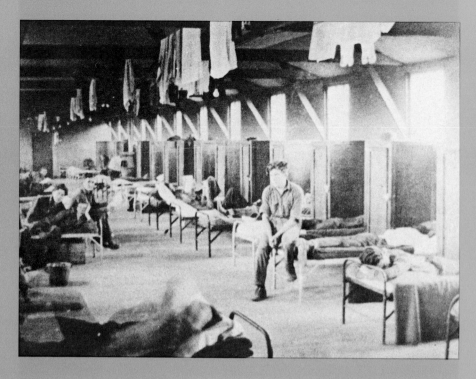

Workers attach minor parts to one of the Fort Mott shore guns, which has been placed in a trunnion bed. The date is March 7, 1898.
Photograph from the Harvey R. Woodlin collection

The exact date of this parade in Woodstown is not known, but the occasion is believed to be a celebration of the end of World War I. Almost two thousand men from Salem County either volunteered for duty in World War I or were drafted. Of that number, thirty-one were killed in action and twenty-four died of disease, principally influenza/pneumonia. Also serving during the war from Salem County were nine nurses and two chaplains. County residents subscribed nearly $7 million to the various Victory Loan drives held beginning in June 1917.
Photograph from the Sam H. Jones collection

The young men of Company 1225 of the Civilian Conservation Corps, most of whom would soon be soldiers fighting in World War II, took photos of each other (pictures one and two). Unfor-

tunately, the persons in the pictures have not been identified. In 1983, the boys of the late thirties returned as senior citizens for an anniversary party (picture three).

Photographs from the Parvin State Park Appreciation Committee collection

The raising of horses, mostly for use at racetracks in the Middle Atlantic states, has become a big business in South Jersey, including Salem County. Some of the finest horses in the county have been raised by Arthur Gemberling of Pilesgrove Township. The white horse, in particular, has won most of the races in which it has been entered.
Photograph by Stephan Harrison

They Who Rediscovered Rural Life

As a girl growing up in urban Gloucester City in the shadow of the Walt Whitman Bridge, Lynn Craig occasionally went on summer picnics with her family to the lakes of rural Salem County.

Today, she and her husband, Gilbert, and three teenage daughters live on one of those lakes—Palatine in Pittsgrove Township—because they "wanted some space."

Many people who have been moving into the county in recent years have been looking for "elbow room," said George Robinson, real estate agent with the Pino Agency in Woodstown. They typically come from the Cherry Hill area, North Jersey, or from Philadelphia and its suburbs, said Robinson, and they want more land for gardens or horses or just for looking at. Sometimes, parents are seeking schools that are less crowded, where the children can get to know most of their classmates, and where they might be less likely to get to know drugs.

"They want a more healthy environment," said Robinson.

Of course, the more healthy environment—the rural scene—does not suit everyone. Some "citified" people who have to move here because of new jobs "get bored" when they are this far removed from the culture, entertainment, and social life of a major metropolitan area, said Robinson.

Sometimes it is the young people from urban areas who have the most trouble adapting. The Craig family had been living in Cherry Hill before they moved to Palatine Lake, and Mrs. Craig thought her children were getting "lost in the shuffle" of large schools. But her daughters, while admitting to some disadvantages of a big school system, also miss the advantages of a more varied and enriching curriculum offered by a large school district, more social activities, and a McDonald's close enough to walk to.

The girls were flabbergasted when they learned that the graduating class of 1986 at Schalick High School in Centerton, which they enrolled in that year, numbered less than one hundred—and that was the largest ever. And they were disappointed when they discovered that the school did not offer swimming as a competitive sport.

However, they also found out that people in small towns often can get things done more quickly than people in a city. When the Craig family and a few others suggested to school officials that a swimming team might be a good addition to the sports program, the idea was approved and ninety-eight students initially signed up.

The school board agreed to pay for the team's transportation to the Vineland YMCA pool.

Whereas in the Craig family it was the children who had the most trouble adapting to life in Salem County, in the Gomez family of Mannington Township, it is young Piño who is adapting just fine. Aged seventeen, Piño is in high school and looking forward to training as a carpenter/mason and working in the area. However, his parents, who have lived in Salem County for twenty-five years, talk about returning to their native Puerto Rico in a few years.

Piño spends the summer months working on the Russell and Dante Spina farm on Haines Neck Road, where his father, Agripiño, is foreman for a crew of twenty-five migrant workers who pick squash, radishes, curcumbers, and tomatoes.

The Gomez family, who are in residence at the Spina farm year-round, are no longer migrant workers, but they were once part of the army of seasonal workers from Puerto Rico and elsewhere who came to Salem County in the spring and moved south in the fall. The annual migration began on a large scale after World War II, but the number of migrant workers has decreased markedly in recent years as many county farmers gave up growing crops that required hand labor.

More than two thousand Puerto Ricans and other Hispanic persons have made Salem County their permanent home, according to the Puerto Rican Action Committee. The second and third generations, who are a stable labor force, are beginning to take a more active role in community affairs and local government. "More are getting to know the issues in their community, questioning candidates for office, registering to vote, and voting," said Sonja Colon, executive director of PRAC. "And this is because fewer of the younger people are planning to 'go home' to Puerto Rico."

Although the migrant workers helped greatly to make Salem County farming highly productive and profitable, not all their children choose to remain in agriculture. Young Piño's sister, Gladys Muñoz, is a beautician in Woodstown. Her husband, Julio, works at the Spina farm with her brother and father, but they live in an apartment complex in Penns Grove. Muñoz talks of returning to Puerto Rico, where he was born and raised and where his father recently died and left the family fifty acres of farm land. Of course, Mrs. Muñoz will go with him, but for her the move would not be a return, because she was born here and feels this is her home.

Salem County today is, at the same time, very different from and very similar to the land that the early settlers found and that has been developed and cared for by generations of their descendants, freed blacks, later European immigrants, migrant workers from Puerto Rico, and, most recently, immigrants from southeast Asia.

If you were to stand on the shoulder of Old King's Highway and look west across the Manning-

People who move to Salem County today are often looking for more space and more fresh air and less congestion and pollution. Gilbert and Lynn Craig moved to Palatine Lake out of the Cherry Hill area where life was getting more hectic and their three girls were becoming lost in a very large school system. While the teenage girls find life a little dull at times in the country, they do find that life on the lake also has its advantages (pictures one and two). In picture three, the girls chat about their new friends and their new school, Schalick High School. From the left are Carla, Candy, and Cheryl. Mrs. Craig, who is a nurse in the neo-natal intensive care unit at Newcomb Medical Center in Vineland, serves lemonade to the girls on the spacious deck that overlooks the lake at one end and wooded grounds at the end pictured. Photographs by Stephan Harrison

ton Meadow, or paddle a canoe along Mad Horse Creek, or walk deep into a forest where deer and wild turkeys live, you might wonder if you were seeing it all as John Fenwick had three hundred years earlier.

But if you continued north on Old Kings Highway, you couldn't miss the "For Sale" signs on large tracts of land; if you stood up in your canoe, you would see the cooling tower on Artificial Island; where you emerged from the forest, you would see that farmers' crops are not what they were just a decade or two ago. You also would quickly realize that the horses you see are not destined to work in the fields, and the trees and shrubs lined up row upon row in nurseries are destined to decorate the lawns of new housing developments and condominium complexes in Salem County and far beyond its borders.

Several major developers have shown interest in large land parcels along Old King's Highway in Pilesgrove Township and elsewhere in the county. Hundreds of homes could rise where cows, sheep, horses and cattle now roam, according to Peter Probasco, county agricultural agent, who predicts a gradual "urbanization" of the county.

The prospect of more housing and less open land is not terribly surprising, of course, since it already has occurred in most of northern New Jersey and as close as neighboring Gloucester County. However, the trend in Salem County could be slowed considerably if a master zoning plan for the state being considered in Trenton is ever enacted, which is not at

In the 1930s, this brochure promoted Woodstown as an "old residence community" where parents could raise their children "away from the disadvantages of cities and industrial communities." A pamphlet of the late 1980s could honestly offer the same environment and advantages. While the population has grown, it still numbers less than five thousand, except during sidewalk sale days in the summer and for the annual candlelight tour on the first Friday in December. On that night, people from as far away as Maryland and Pennsylvania trudge up and down the streets and walk through the old residences decorated for Christmas. Brochure from the Sam H. Jones collection

Woodstown

If seeking a home in restful and healthful surroundings—away from the disadvantages of cities and industrial communities, yet within easy touch—consider Woodstown.

An old residence community, dating back to Colonial times; a charming country-seat of shade, lawns, gardens, flowers; back from the coastal lowlands to where the air is pure and invigorating; set amidst rolling hills, and surrounded by sylvan lakes.

Woodstown is the residential center of historic Salem County, and the chosen home of professional and business men of Philadelphia, Wilmington, and those in industries along the Delaware River. Wilmington is but ten miles away; Philadelphia only twenty-four miles. New York is a drive of less than three hours; Baltimore, less; and Atlantic City is an after-supper drive. Woodstown is directly on U. S. Route 40 (Harding Highway), the all hard surface high-way from Atlantic City to San Francisco.

all certain. The plan would establish seven zones, or "tiers," in the state, according to Probasco. The sixth tier, which is the designation for this county, calls for twenty-acre zoning—one dwelling per twenty acres. Such zoning could ensure that the county remains essentially as it is, mostly rural.

Not since the exceptional boom time of the Du Pont plants during World War I has any single event impacted with such force on the population and economy of Salem County as did the arrival of three nuclear power plants in the 1970s and 1980s. Today, the nuclear energy complex operated by the Public Service Electric & Gas Company on Artificial Island in Lower Alloways Creek is the second largest such facility in the country.

In 1985, when PSE&G was completing work on the Hope Creek plant, the last of the three plants constructed, at least ten thousand persons were employed at Artificial Island. Even now, it takes nearly two thousand persons to operate the plants daily; another eight hundred consultants and contractors are employed regularly. One thousand persons are hired for periods of four to eight weeks to perform certain kinds of specialized tasks, such as refueling.

PSE&G has joined with Du Pont, Mannington Mills, and Atlantic Electric (which operates a conventional power plant at the base of the Delaware Memorial Bridge) to form a private corporation known as Stand Up for Salem. The group is promoting the revitalization of the city of Salem, according to Richard A. Silverio, community affairs manager for PSE&G. The four companies were expected to present an action plan before the end of 1988.

If the crops of county farmers are not what they were a decade or so ago, they are more in keeping with the crops of perhaps two hundred years ago. The huge vegetable farms that once covered the land are now mostly gone—along with the processing plants, except for the Seabrook frozen vegetable plant in nearby Bridgeton (Cumberland County). Many of the farmers have returned to field crops. Of course, today's major field crop in the county is the soybean (twenty-one thousand acres in 1985), which wasn't even grown in the United States until the early 1800s, but the next two most important crops in terms of acreage, corn (twelve-thousand acres) and hay (six thousand acres), also were key crops in the 1700s.

Field crops could become even greater sources of income for local farmers if Salem Municipal Port is successful in selling or leasing its grain elevator to a company or farmers' cooperative. The port, which had fallen on hard times since the early 1900s, was resuscitated in 1982. One of the first shipments out of the "new" port was fifteen hundred tons of soybeans grown by seven county farmers. It was the first time in a century that a field crop had been shipped out of any New Jersey port.

More than two years later, forty bargeloads of soybeans, valued at $4 million, were floated down Salem River to the Delaware, and the fifteen thousand metric tons of soybeans were transferred to a Spanish freighter anchored in the Delaware. But such a midstream transfer operation is expensive, and while farmers gained, the port lost money.

Blanch I. Hogate, supervisor of accounts for the Municipal Port Authority, said the Authority is

The public schools in the city of Salem were not integrated until after World War II. The Grant School (no longer standing) was for black children. This picture, taken in early 1940s, shows the school's principal and staff. Standing in front, from left to right, are Margaret Scott, Alice Warnick, and Elizabeth Cline. In the second row are Principal Charles Gries and Jennie Jackson. The teachers in the third row are, from the left, P. F. Alton Jordan, Lydia Sheetz, Helen Lindsey, and James Rice. Photograph from the Today's Sunbeam *collection*

131

anxious to resume shipping home-grown soybeans and other field crops using the grain elevator, which can put the product directly on ships, rather than on barges for later transfer. Also in the future, larger ships, like the Spanish freighter that took on Salem crops while anchored in the Delaware River, may be able to move up the Salem River to dock at the grain elevator. The Port Authority expects dredging of the Salem River to a depth of eighteen feet to begin in 1990. The current depth is fourteen feet.

There also exists a bright future for people who don't want to use the land either for growing crops, grazing dairy cows and cattle, or building housing developments.

According to the 1987 Equine Survey published by the state Department of Agriculture, the county stands eighth among the twenty-one counties in the number of acres devoted to the raising of horses (thirteen thousand). Most of the horses are raised for the many race tracks in the northeastern and middle Atlantic states.

County Agricultural Agent Pete Probasco foresees a significant increase in the number of sod farms (turf industry) and nurseries in the county.

The nursery business, especially, could adapt very well to the urbanization he predicts. Whereas one hundred acres would not be much of a soybean farm, said Probasco, it would do nicely for a nursery.

Almost anything written today about Salem County's tomorrows is subject to change without notice. Who knows for certain what industries may transform the county in the twenty-first century. Will Salem become mostly a home base for men and women commuting to work in the Wilmington and Philadelphia Metropolitan Areas? Will the county become the turf and nursery capital of the East Coast, its sod and ornamental trees adorning lawns and gardens in southern Connecticut and northern Virginia?

One thing is certain, though, the future, as always, will be decided by people. And so far, the county has been in good hands, whether they belonged to the troubled Quaker John Fenwick, the former slave John Rock, the duPont brothers, or the farm foreman Agripiño Gomez. In the end, we have no other choice than to entrust Salem County to the hands of yet unborn generations. ■

Agripiño Gomez (picture one) has worked on the Spina farm in Mannington Township for the past twenty-five years, but plans eventually to return to Puerto Rico. However, his son, Piño (at left in picture two) probably will remain here after he finishes high school. In the foreground of picture two is Dante Spina, who is washing yellow squash in preparation for crating. Picture three shows workers bringing in squash just picked in the field. In the background (behind the truck) is Julio Muñoz, whose wife, Gladys, is a beautician in Woodstown. The man on the truck is Juan Muñoz, a cousin of Julio's. The Gomez and Muñoz families, once migratory, are now part of the county's stable labor force. Picture four shows workers on the Spina farm picking radishes. The Puerto Rican Action Committee reports that it is common now for meetings having to do with community issues to bring out large numbers of Puerto Rican and other Hispanic residents of the county (picture five). Dr. Leonard Fitts, superintendent of schools in Penns Grove, is in the front row at right.
Photographs one through four by Stephan Harrison; photograph five from the Puerto Rican Action Committee collection

The first trolley to run in Pennsville (they do not run any longer) is shown here beginning its maiden trip in 1917. Photograph from the Sam H. Jones collection

In 1922, President Warren G. Harding came to Woodstown to dedicate the Harding Highway. Here he addresses the crowd from the steps of the Woodstown High School. Most of the Harding Highway today is Route 40, although the western portion of it is Route 48 running into Penns Grove. Photograph from the Sam H. Jones collection

Before the Delaware Memorial Bridge spanned the great river in the 1960s, people and vehicles crossed between Salem county and New Castle and Wilmington, Delaware, by ferryboat. The boats left docks in Penns Grove and Pennsville.
Photograph from the Today's Sunbeam *collection*

The last steam-driven train from Salem left the city the day after Christmas in 1950. In charge were four men. They are, from left to right: Robert Barrett, brakeman; Walter F. Diament, conductor; R. F. Penn, fireman; and Samuel Powers, engineer.
Photograph from the Today's Sunbeam *collection*

The battleship New Jersey *moves downriver in 1968 under the Delaware Memorial Bridge, which connects Deepwater in Salem County with Swanwyck, just south of Wilmington, Delaware. The bridge also carries most of the north-south traffic on the east coast. In this picture, the second span (foreground) is not quite finished. Photograph from the Sam H. Jones collection*

The country store in Alloway (picture one) operated today by Robert P. Dorrell and his wife was first used as a store in 1838, although the building goes back before that date. The little office in the store (picture two) holds a vast number of old books, pictures, and papers regarding the history of the area. For example, the minutes of the annual meeting of the Haines Neck Marsh Company (later the Haines Neck Meadow Company) going back to the 1830s are on file. The company, which built sluices for farmers, evidently was not a big operation even by early nineteenth-century standards. In 1832, the company expended all of $77.01. The third picture shows Mrs. Dorrell (right) waiting on a customer. Despite the sign in the upper right corner of the picture, muskrat meat is no longer for sale. The last picture shows a display of handmade mugs, each bearing the name of a Salem County town.

Photographs by Stephan Harrison

It's auction day in Alloway! Robert P. Dorrell, with back to camera, is in charge. Auctions are common in Salem County, whether they are selling farm animals and equipment or houses, outbuildings and personal property belonging to an old family without descendants who can or will inherit them. Photograph from the Robert P. Dorrell collection

The flags of the United States and a number of other countries fly over ships that continue a centuries-old tradition of making the city of Salem a port of call. Picture two shows the ship Emerald Icechest, a 210-foot long ship, which in the spring of 1988, has just unloaded spices, hearts of palm, Brazil nuts and lumber from Antigua and other Caribbean islands. The port from across Salem River is seen in picture three. The grain elevator, which could boost the profits for county farmers (picture four), is awaiting a new owner and needed repairs. Rail service to the port enables goods to be shipped from the dock either by train or truck (picture five). Photographs by Stephan Harrison

Trapping has been an important occupation in the county since the days of the Lenape Indians. When you talk about trapping in Salem County, you are talking mostly about catching muskrats in the marshes along the Delaware River. Although beaver have been trapped from the time of the first settlers, and also fox and raccoon, it is the muskrat that has been most sought after and its fur sold commercially. The first picture shows trappers standing in front of one of the men's homes on Hope Creek in 1912. Muskrat pelts are drying in the attic of Warren Davis' house in picture two; the time is the same. Trappers John M. Pancoast, Ben Kates, and Isaac Brandiff stand in front of their cabin in the late 1800s or early 1900s (third picture). Part of their catch is hanging on the wall at left. Photographs one and two by William J. S. Bradway from the Lower Alloways Creek collection; photograph three from the Salem County Historical Society collection

The year is 1988, and Calvin Hill of Canton, (picture one) trapper and owner of the Silver Lake Fur Company, shows off pelts of muskrat, fox, and raccoon. In the second picture, Hill stands in front of his collection of duck decoys. At his feet is a box trap similar to the one "ratters" use today because of a recent state law that prohibits the use of the steel-jaw leg-trap. The box-trap and snare allowed by law are not as effective as the old trap, said Hill. "It's like the toilet seat," he explained. "No one has ever come up with anything better." The catch varies from season to season (the trapping season runs from December 1 to March 15). Hill and two other men caught thirty-six hundred "rats" in 1987-1988, whereas he and five other trappers caught ten thousand the previous season. Environmental changes can affect the catch.
Photographs by Stephan Harrison

For more than fifty years, the lower Alloways Creek has sponsored an annual muskrat dinner attended by as many as five hundred persons, who consume two thousand or so "rats" in four sittings. The meat is prepared and cooked by the firemen, and the process starts at least ten days before the first sitting. The "rats" are cleaned by soaking them in water, rinsing, and then soaking them again. The meat is then frozen until two days before the dinner, when it is taken out to thaw. The day before the dinner, the meat is cut into pieces about the size of stewing beef and boiled, along with a few onions and salt, for three to four minutes. Just before the dinner begins, the cooked meat is deep fried to "brown and heat it up." In picture two, John Heller of Harmersville measures out a portion of muskrat for his plate.
Photographs from the Today's Sunbeam *collection*

*Salem County Memorial Hospital was located on Market Street in Salem during the 1930s when this picture was taken. The hospital was relocated in the 1950s to property in Mannington Township, and later additions have made it a modern medical complex.
Photograph from the B. Harold Smick, Jr. collection*

The future for agriculture in Salem County is supposed to include nurseries and sod farms. Victor Scott, who lives in a house that is almost three hundred years old, is getting ready for that tomorrow. Scott owns the three hundred-acre South Jersey Colonial Nurseries in Mannington Township, and he recently purchased a modern tree digger (picture one) that can dig up and lift on to a flatbed truck a large-size tree. Also, Scott is converting his nursery from what he calls horse rows. Back in 1955, when he started the business, nurseries still planted trees and shrubs in horse rows, which means three feet apart (picture two). Today's modern equipment demands rows that are twelve feet apart, said Scott. His nursery sells to landscape architects and building contractors in an eight-state area.
Photographs by Stephan Harrison

The Salem Generating Station, which consists of three nuclear power plants, is located on Artificial Island, a man-made peninsula three miles long and one mile wide along the shore of Lower Alloways Creek Township. Only one cooling tower was built, because the other two plants are cooled by water from the Delaware River. Public Service Electric & Gas completed the Salem I plant in 1976 and the Salem II plant in 1981. The Hope Creek facility was finished in 1986. One picture shows the refueling floor of the containment building in the Hope Creek plant. The open reactor is in the center of the picture. A refueling technician, in white coat and hat, is seen in another picture. The last picture shows a control room supervisor, the person who watches over the many panels of dials, switches, and lights.
Photographs from PSE&G

Mannington Mills, built along Fenwick's Creek (at right in overview), is one of the county's major industries. The sixty buildings cover 31 acres of a 328-acre site. One of the early buildings is seen in picture two. The company, *which is still owned by the Campbell family, had its start in 1915 in a plant in Salem. It was in 1922 that Mannington Mills occupied its current location in Mannington Township. John B. Campbell II, the current chairman of* *the board, is the grandson of the company's founder.*
Photographs from the Mannington Mills collection

At the Chicago Trade Market in 1958, Mannington Mills "shocked" the industry by displaying a new product: twelve-foot-wide rotogravure printed vinyl sheets. The vinyl sheets were printed in a fashion similar to the pages of a newspaper or magazine. Mannington Mills still prints sheet vinyl (picture one), but now its subsidiaries also produce wood, carpet, and ceramic tile floor covering. In 1978, a new corporate headquarters was built and added to in 1986. The corporate headquarters includes a physical fitness center open to all employees (picture two).

Photographs from the Mannington Mills collection

It surprises most new Salem County residents and visitors, and even some long-time residents, to learn that the county is dotted with more then one hundred homes dating to the seventeenth and eighteenth centuries. One of the oldest is this house on Compromise Road in Mannington Township. The original portion of the house, at right in picture one, was built by Samuel Hedge, who arrived in 1675 with John Fenwick and soon after landing married Fenwick's daughter, Anna. The house is believed to be the only one in the county that has additions from four centuries, starting, of course, with the original section in the 1600s. The second picture taken from the side of the house, shows some of the later additions. The current owners of the home and spacious grounds are Mr. and Mrs. Dean C. Pappas.
Photographs by Stephan Harrison

Redroe Morris purchased this house on the Delaware River in Elsinboro from Samuel Carpenter in 1688 (picture one). The house has changed little in three centuries as picture two illustrates. The man and child standing by the water's edge in the old photo are not identified, but the two men looking out through the fog on a spring day in 1988 are the present owner, Benjamin C. Harris and Joseph J. McCarthy, who rents an apartment in the house. Photograph one from the Salem County Historical Society collection; photograph two by Stephan Harrison

One hundred years ago, from 1887 to 1889, a local photographer, Thomas J. Yorke, took pictures of some of the county's pre-Revolutionary War homes, then already one or two centuries old. He noted at the time that they were still being lived in, and in many cases the nineteenth-century owners were direct descendants of the original builders. Some of the homes photographed by Yorke were re-photographed in the late 1980s, and they are still lived in and enjoyed. Of course, many buildings have been modified and added to over the years, but some changes were made even before their original owners had died. This picture of Yorke is from the same time period as the pictures themselves. He was forty-four years old. The Yorke pictures are from the Salem County Historical Society collection

152

According to the Salem County Historical Society, the Richard Johnson house at One Johnson Street in the city of Salem is the "oldest standing dwelling" in the county. The original clapboard house, which is the left portion of the building in each picture, was built in 1687 by the senior Richard Johnson, who came here from England a few months after John Fenwick. A descendant of Richard Johnson was Col. Robert G. Johnson, who has been featured in the narrative of this book (Chapter IV). Colonel Johnson, however, never lived in the house. Apparently, when the trees shown in front of the house in the Yorke picture were taken down and the street graded and paved, it was necessary to build steps up to the porch. The brick addition was build in 1840. The present owners of the house are Mr. and Mrs. Allen J. Carrel. The 1988 photograph by Stephan Harrison

The date of the Isaac Smart house on the Fort Elfsborg-Salem Road in Elsinboro is the subject of some good-natured debate. The Salem County Historical Society puts the original date of construction at 1689, but the present owners, the Champion Coles family, claim the earliest construction, that portion with the double chimney at the right side in both pictures, goes back to 1683. The Coleses also point to the date of 1697 that is written into the brick over the door to the other portion of the house. While this is the front of the house in both the 1888 and 1988 pictures, it was the rear of the house when it was first built (date unknown). Most early houses faced a navigable creek or river because those were the routes of transportation then. After reasonably good roads were built, homeowners adapted to the new mode of transportation by making their back door the front door and vice versa. The Coles family can walk out their back door today and, within two hundred or so feet reach a

stream connecting to the nearby Delaware River.
The 1988 photograph by Stephan Harrison

154

The William Hall, Jr. house is located on the Woodstown-Salem Road, and the original portion (on the left side in the pictures) was built in 1724. The house is now owned by Donald Emel, but it is his parents, Mr. and Mrs. Roland Emel, who purchased the house in 1926 and still live there. The house remains the hub of a working farm. Again, it must be noted that this was once the rear of the house when no Woodstown-Salem Road existed and transportation was by way of Nichomus Run (named for a Lenape Indian chief) that still runs sluggishly across what once was the front of the property. The 1988 photograph by Stephan Harrison

John Fenwick gave a land grant to Samuel Nicholson in 1675, while both men still were in England, but Nicholson did not build this house until 1752, a number of years after he emigrated from England. The house is now owned by Mr. and Mrs. Harold Smick, Jr., who call the place Amwellbury Farm. It is located on Amwellbury Road in Elsinboro.
The 1988 photograph by Stephan Harrison

The John Maddox Denn house, built in 1725, is located a quarter mile or so west of the Hancock house on Poplar Street in Hancock's Bridge, Lower Alloways Creek Township. After the British massacre of American militiamen sleeping in the Hancock House in 1778, some of the wounded, including old William Hancock, were brought to this house for treatment. It was here that Hancock died.
The 1988 photograph by Stephan Harrison

The Ware-Shourds house, just down the road from the Denn house and on the south bank of Alloways Creek, was constructed in 1730 by Joseph Ware, Jr. He was the son of a man who was a servant to Edward Wade, a member of the first party of English settlers brought here by John Fenwick. The first Joseph Ware must have saved every cent he earned as a servant (and perhaps married well), because in little more than a decade after his arrival he had sufficient funds to purchase 250 acres from his former master and an equal parcel from another landowner. In the 1800s, the house was bought by Thomas Shourds, one of the county's first published historians (History and Genealogy of Fenwick's Colony in 1876). The current owners are the David Campbells. The house is at the end of a long driveway off Poplar Street in Hancock's Bridge, and the front (shown in both pictures) still faces Alloways Creek.

The 1988 photograph by Stephan Harrison

Benjamin Holme purchased this house on Fort Elfsborg Road in Elsinboro in 1762 from the half brother of David

Morris, who constructed the original building in 1729. Holme was a colonel of militia during the American Revolution. Because of this position, the building was burned and severely damaged by British soldiers in 1778. Holme rebuilt the house after the war. The first Mrs. Holme died soon after their marriage and the couple had no children. After the war, Holme married Esther Gibbon, whose first husband had died in a British prison ship in New York harbor. Holme met Mrs. Gibbon when she came to his house to tell him that while she was in New York attending to her husband's affairs she saw a grandfather's clock with Holme's name on it in the British officers' quarters. The clock now chimes the hours at the Salem County Historical Society building. The present owners of "Holmeland" are Mr. and Mrs. Brian Duffy.
The 1988 photograph by Stephan Harrison

The Dickinson house on Brickyard Road in Alloway Township is considered to have the finest display of glazed brick in the county. The decorative brickwork includes the initials of the original owners, the date of construction (1754), and highly intricate and artistic design. Photographs by Stephan Harrison

Many old homes have been added on to or modernized in some way but, essentially, the structures remain pretty much as they were when first constructed by early settlers. One example is the Abbott house, which was built in 1704 by George Abbott on the north side of Alloways Creek in Elsinboro. Today, it is the home of Superior Court Judge and Mrs. George Farrell. The first picture shows what originally was the front of the house, with additions, when transportation was more apt to be by boat on Alloways Creek than by road. Except for new furnishings and modernizing in the kitchen, the downstairs living area in the original house looks much the same as it did when the British occupied it in March 1778. Photographs by Stephan Harrison

This house on Route 40 in Pilesgrove Township, recently restored, now resembles the same house as it appeared in a lithograph of the mid-1800s. In Salem County, few old homes are bulldozed for parking lots and shopping malls. In most cases, people buy them, restore them, and live in them. Recently, Woodstown created a historic district so that homes dating to the eighteenth and nineteenth centuries would be preserved for the future.
Photograph by Stephan Harrison

Plenty of open land still exists in the county, and it is still less expensive per acre than in most counties of New Jersey. However, more and more farm acreage may be disappearing in the future as people move farther and farther away from urban areas such as Philadelphia, Camden, and Cherry Hill to the north. These fields along King's Highway in Pilesgrove Township were being considered for luxury homes and a private country club.
Photograph by Stephan Harrison

Bull Dogging

BULLDOGGING of today is an evolution of a difficult feat started years ago when Will Pickett, of Taylor, Texas, thrilled and startled the rodeo world by leaping from his horse to the horns of a running steer and then throwing him without the use of hands. A local paper of August 30, 1904, describing this event says, "He sank his strong ivory teeth into the under lip of the animal and throwing his shoulder against the neck of the steer, strained and twisted until the brute, under the strain of the slowly bending neck, sank to the ground."

Today bulldogging is an entirely different event, though equally difficult and dangerous. The steer is given a thirty-foot start on the contestant, who together with an assistant called a "hazer" attempts to keep the steer running straight ahead. The bulldogger leaps from his horse, grabbing the steer by the horns and after bringing it to a stop, twists it down. If steer is accidentally knocked or thrown down before being brought to a stop, it must be let up on four feet and then thrown. The steer will be considered down only when it is lying flat on its side, all four feet out and head straight.

Purse $300.00. Day Monies $20.00—$10.00. Entrance fee $20.00. Total entrance fees go for best total time. Split 50% for 1st; 30% for 2nd, and 20% for 3rd.

Courtesy of HOWEY'S SERVICE STATION
Pontiac Agency, Phone 195, Woodstown

TOM PERKINS BULLDOGGING
Salem County Rodeo, 1935

Stoney Harris' rodeo was as popular in August of 1936, when this program was printed, as it is today. Bull dogging is now called steer wrestling, but the cowboy still must hop off his horse and grab the steer's horns when both animals are racing at about thirty miles per hour.
Brochure from the Sam H. Jones collection

Salem County is mostly known outside its boundaries not as the home of a huge Du Pont complex, not as the site of the second largest nuclear power complex in the country, and not as a halfway stop between Baltimore and the Atlantic City casinos. What it is mostly known for is the Cowtown Rodeo, located on Route 40 in Pilesgrove Township. Cowtown is the only weekly rodeo during the summer months (every Saturday night) east of the Mississippi River. People—a lot of families—nearly fill the four thousand-seat stadium (wooden bleachers) for each performance (pictures one and two). They come mostly from New Jersey, Pennsylvania, Delaware, and Maryland, but a stroll through the parking area will spot license plates on cars and campers from all over the country. The rodeo has been featured on national television at least four times. Cowboy attire is almost as common on people in the stands as it is on the participants (picture three). Each performance begins with live country music (picture four). A recent spectator, seeing the rodeo for the first time, looked around as the music began and the cowboys and cowgirls lined up for the opening ceremonies and remarked, "You would never dream you were in New Jersey—or on the east coast for that matter."
Photographs by Stephan Harrison

The Cowtown Rodeo has been operated by the Harris family of Pilesgrove Township since its founding in 1929. Howard Grant Harris is the current owner; he also is an accomplished rodeo competitor. Cowtown is affiliated with the Professional Rodeo Cowboys Association and presents the same events one would find at a rodeo in Montana or anywhere else on the professional circuit: bareback riding (pictures one and two), calf roping (picture three), saddle bronc riding, steer wrestling, bull riding, team roping, and girls' barrel racing. When it comes to bareback riding and saddle bronc riding, the cowboy is lucky if he is helped to the ground by rodeo officials riding in the

ring (picture four), rather than thrown off by his horse. The cowboy who just completed a successful ride is Buck Howard of Penns Grove. The cowboy also has a friend in the ring in the person of the rodeo clown. Although the clown entertains the audience, he also helps prevent injuries to cowboys. Steve Jones of Millersville, Maryland, is the Cowtown Rodeo clown (picture five). According to Tim Toulson of Alloway, who has "been with horses" all his life, but is new to the rodeo, a cowboy can earn "a couple of thousand dollars in a summer" at Cowtown if he's really good.

Photographs by Stephan Harrison

Bibliography

Chapter I
Articles

Kraft, Herbert C. "The Northern Lenape in Prehistoric and Early Colonial Times." *The Lenape Indian: A Symposium* (Archaeological Research Center, Seton Hall University, South Orange, N.J.), (1984).

Morris, George J. " A Preliminary Investigation of the Osborn Site, Salem County, New Jersey." *Bulletin of the Archaeological Society of New Jersey* (Seton Hall University, South Orange, N.J.) 38 (1982).

Revey, James "Lone Bear." "The Delaware Indians in New Jersey, from Colonial Times to the Present." *The Lenape Indian: A Symposium* (Archaeological Research Center, Seton Hall University, South Orange, N.J.), (1984).

Williams, Lorriane E. and Thomas, Ronald A. "The Early/Middle Woodland Period in New Jersey: ca. 1000 B.C.-A.D. 1000." *New Jersey's Archaeological Resources* (Office of New Jersey Heritage, Trenton, N.J.), (1982).

Books

Stewart, Frank H. *Indians of Southern New Jersey*. Woodbury, N.J.: N.p., 1932.

Chapter II
Books

Fenwick's Colony. Salem, N.J.: The Salem County Tercentenary Committee, 1964.

Leiby, Adrian C. *The Early Dutch and Swedish Settlers of New Jersey*. Princeton, N.J.: D. Van Nostrand Company, Inc., 1964.

Sickler, Joseph S. *History of Salem*. Salem, N.J.: Sunbeam Publishing Company, 1937.

Stewart, Frank H. *Major John Fenwick*. Salem, N.J.: Salem County Historical Society, 1964.

Van Name, Elmer Garfield. *Anthony Nelson: Seventeenth Century Pennsylvania and New Jersey and Some of His Descendants*. Haddonfield, N.J.: N.p., 1962.

Pamphlets

New Sweden '88: The Significance of Swedish and Finnish Settlement in the Delaware Valley. Trenton, N.J.: New Sweden Commemorative Commission, 1988.

Primary Source Material:Report of Governor Johan Printz. Trenton, N.J.: New Sweden Commemorative Commission, 1988.

The Way it Used to Be, Vol. I, No. 2. Salem, N.J.: Salem County Cultural and Heritage Commission, April 1975.

Chapter III
Articles

"Old South Jersey Glass". *Almanac and Year Book* (First National Bank of Woodstown, Woodstown, N.J.) (1920).

Sinnickson, Lloyd. " St. George's Episcopal Church". Salem County Historical Society *Newsletter 32* (March 1987).

Talley, Louisa E. " St. Joseph's Church, Woodstown". Salem County Historical Society *Newsletter 31* (June 1986).

Books

Alloway Remembers. 2d Ed. Pitman, N.J.: Alloway Township Bicentennial of the Constitution Committee, 1988.

Johnson, R. G. *First Settlement of Salem*. Philadelphia: Orrin Rogers, 1839.

The Records of the Swedish Lutheran Churches of Raccoon and Penns Neck, 1713-1786. Federal Writers Project of the Works Progress Administration. Elizabeth, N.J.: Cobly and McGowan, Inc., 1928.

Sickler, Joseph S. *History of Salem*. Salem, N.J.: Sunbeam Publishing Company, 1937

Stewart, Frank H. *Salem County in the Revolution*. Salem, N.J.: Salem Country Historical Society, 1967.

Chapter IV
Articles

"Choose Ye This Day Whom Ye Will Serve." *National Standard & Salem County Advertiser*. (Salem, N.J.), (April 17, 1861).

Books

A History of a Food Processor. Williamstown, N.J. Violet Packing Company, 1978.

Alloway Remembers. 2d Ed. Alloway, N.J.: Alloway Township Bicentennial of the Constitution Committee, 1988.

Chew, William H. *Salem County Handbook*. Salem, N.J.: Salem National Banking Company, 1924.

Cushing, Thomas. *History of Gloucester, Salem and Cumberland Counties*. Philadelphia: Charles E. Sheppard, Everts & Peck, 1883.

Encyclopaedia Britannica. Vol 11. Chicago, Ill.: Encyclopaedia Britannica, Inc., 1986.

Fenwick's Colony. Salem, N.J.: The Salem County Tercentenary Committee, 1964.

Lossing, Benson, J. *Our Country*. Vol 2. New York: Henry J. Johnson, 1800.

Nathan, Mark A. *A Bicentennial History of Public Education in Salem County, New Jersey*. Salem, N.J.: Salem County Board of Freeholders, 1976.

Pingeon, Frances D. *Blacks in the Revolutionary Era*. Trenton, N.J.: New Jersey Historical Commission, 1975.

Price, Clement Alexander. *Freedom Not Far Distant*. Newark, N.J.: New Jersey Historical Society, 1980.

Salem County Heritage. Salem, N.J.: Salem County Planning Board, 1967.

Shourds, Thomas. *History and Genealogy of Fenwick's Colony. Bridgeton, N.J.*: George F. Nixon, 1876.

Sickler, Joseph S. *History of Salem*. Salem, N.J.: Sunbeam Publishing Company, 1937.

The Way It Used to Be. Vols. 1 and 2. Salem, N.J.: Salem County Cultural and Heritage Commission, 1975.

Chapter V
Articles

" Bustling Explosives Plant Obscured Birth of Orchem Unit Here". *The Chambers Works News* (Deepwater, N.J.), (February 1, 1967).

"Dr. Chambers Sparked Dye Venture". *The Chambers Works News* (Deepwater, N.J.), (April 1967).

" Du Pont's Orchem Industry Born Here In 1917." *The Chambers Works News* (Deepwater, N.J.), (January 1967).

The Carney Pointer. Series of articles running from May 1951 to October-November 1952 (Carney's Point, N.J.).

Books

Fenwick's Colony. Salem, N.J.: Salem County Tercentenary Committee, 1964.

Sickler, Joseph S. *History of Salem*. Salem, N.J: Sunbeam Publishing Company, 1937.

Chapter VI
Articles

"Horses play major role in county" *Today's Sunbeam*; Salem, N.J.; June 10, 1988.

"Layton's Lake Estates site plan changes due soon." *Today's Sunbeam* (Salem, N.J.), (May 3, 1988).

Books

Fenwick's Colony. Salem, N.J.: Salem County Tercentenary Committee, 1964.

Sickler, Joseph S. *History of Salem*. Salem, N.J.: Sunbeam Publishing Company, 1937.

Pamphlets

"Chronological History of the Salem Municipal Port Project." Salem, N.J.: City of Salem Municipal Port Authority, N.d.

"Nuclear Energy." Hancock's Bridge, N.J.: Public Service Electric & Gas Company, N.d.

"Port Review." Salem, N.J.: City of Salem Municipal Port Authority, January 1988.

Index